SPELLCRAFT

A PRACTICAL GUIDE TO MAGIC

SILVER RAVEN

SIRIUS

SIRIUS

This edition published in 2024 by Sirius Publishing, a division of
Arcturus Publishing Limited,
26/27 Bickels Yard, 151–153 Bermondsey Street,
London SE1 3HA

All images courtesy of Shutterstock

ISBN: 978-1-3988-4341-7
AD010765UK

Printed in China

CONTENTS

INTRODUCTION

Power is something that we all crave. Not in the sense of wanting to subjugate others (or at least I hope not!), but in the sense of having control over our lives. Why do we strive to get ahead in career and business? It is not just for the financial gain, it is also for the status of being senior enough to have agency over our working lives. In our relationships, we often wish we could telepathically discover what the other person is thinking. As we move through an occasionally combative world, we would be helped with the sort of intuitive knowledge that those with witchy powers seem to have. As we navigate our lives, wouldn't it be wonderful to have some extra help in the form of supernatural skills?

Since the start of recorded history, humans have attempted to affect the world around them. Whether this was in praying to deities for nature to be kind and food to be plentiful or shamanic journeying to gain guidance and healing before the birth of modern medicine, we wanted to empower ourselves. While some of the ideas behind the spells in modern Western witchcraft are fairly modern, our human connection to ritual goes back to the birth of civilization.

From the highly theatrical ritual of high magic—the sort of magic you'd find in the Western Esoteric Tradition whereby a magician or coven might attempt to practice magic for the sake of elevating consciousness in the world—to the folk magic that is practiced throughout the world by shamans, witches and healers, it is clear that spellcrafting is all around us.

In terms of my own tradition, it is centered in the Indian subcontinent. I have practiced magic for more than fifty years now and this book rounds up all of the most potent spellcraft that I have learned over the years. All the techniques here have been tried-and-tested over several years. However, as you progress in your own magical journey, you will find that some things work better for you and your energy make-up than others. That is absolutely fine and you should trust yourself to know what works best for you.

The magic I practice does not follow one specific tradition. This is because I am a first-generation immigrant and many traditions require you to have a connection with the land in which you practice or with the land from which the tradition comes. I have lived most of my life in Britain. However, I also have a global outlook

and a purely English practice of magic does not honor my ancestors or those teachers I have met from other parts of the world. As such, I have an unapologetically eclectic approach to magical work. Therefore, you will find here spells and magical charms from all over the world. I hope that you will find comfort and joy in discovering the magic and enchantment that is all around you. As you gain confidence, create your own spells inspired either by what is here or by your own innate magical powers. We all have wonder and magic as our birthright so feel free to explore what spells and charms can do for you.

The title *Spellcraft* relates to the fact that magic is a craft and an art that you improve on as you deepen your practice over the years. We also use charms in this book as part of spellwork. The word charm has Latin origins in the word *carmen* meaning "song" or "chant," and some witches believe that a truly potent spell should have a verbal component. I am not strict about that as I have seen powerful spells enacted in silence, whether in the performance of a magical act or written down in a talisman of some sort. As always, you must go with what feels correct to you and your spirit.

Charms, in their medieval usage, were broad in that the word could mean a magical incantation or a written spell or magical recipe. It was also taken to mean putting someone or something under a spell or enchantment.

Stones and small trinkets have been found from the Neolithic era that suggest that those Neolithic tribes believed in spellcraft in the sense that they possibly carried such items with them as good luck tokens, perhaps to help in hunts at a time when life must have seemed difficult and brutish without some supernatural help. A modern witch might tie a blue ribbon around her phone in the office to facilitate better communication and attract greater prosperity through calls that lead to a good financial outcome. Such small uses of charms and tokens is also an important part of spellcrafting and should not be dismissed as too simple to count as magic.

Once you get into the swing of things, you may find that all your days fizzle with the excitement of magic—even if some people erroneously interpret all the signs as coincidences or synchronicities. Don't waste your time trying to convince them. Spellcrafting is not an evangelical process. Of course, with permission, you can do spells and make charms for friends and family, but you are not required to "convert" anyone to your way of thinking.

Some examples of spellcrafting through the ages can be seen when we look at practices to ward off evil and attract luck. These include the witch-bottles that have been found buried in hearths throughout the British Isles and America (used to ward off evil spirits), the *taweez* (protective amulet) worn by many in the Indian subcontinent, the *tcherot* (meaning paper to refer to talismanic notes hidden inside the amulet) of the Tuareg people of northern Africa, and the yansheng coins of China. There are many more all over the world. Even as we move into more secular times, we retain a belief in good or bad luck and, on occasion, even the most cynical among us will avoid certain practices said to be unlucky, such as walking under ladders.

We will begin by looking at the energetic magic that keeps us protected in our daily lives. This starts off with preparing yourself and your space to ensure the optimum conditions for beginning to work with spells. You will discover the basics of your energy make-up and how to work safely with energy as well as the principles of repelling and attracting outcomes. You will also learn rituals to keep your energy clear regularly and how to nourish yourself so that you are in the best place to do this work.

Then we will look at how to use specific spells for each outcome and you will learn how to trust your own intuition when preparing a spell or a charm to be worn, displayed or used in a ritual.

Finally, we will look at how to ensure that your spells continue to work and what it means when one is not working. You will begin to understand how spells work and learn how to make ones that will work for you alone.

Step into your personal power with the practices and rituals contained within this book. Learn how to balance and strengthen your energy so that you can deal with anything that modern living throws at you.

HOW TO BEGIN

1

HARNESSING ENERGY

Before starting any magical work, it's essential to cleanse both your personal energy and the energy of where you'll be doing your spellwork. This goes beyond physical cleanliness; it involves purifying the invisible energies around you and your space. Skipping this crucial step can lead to ineffective spells, tainted by negative thought forms, stagnant energies, and past negative experiences. At best, this will render your spellwork powerless; at worst, it may produce the opposite of your intended effect. However, with regular practice, you'll find that both your energy and your space's energy become stronger and more protective, allowing you to quickly achieve the right mindset for magic. In this section, we will explore the ingredients, tools, and practices used for energetic cleansing.

TOOLKIT FOR ENERGY CLEANSING

- Salts: see the list opposite for the varieties and what they do
- a natural wood brush or besom
- a bowl used just for ritual purposes
- some incense

WHICH MOON PHASE?

Some witches believe that all banishing or removal spells (for example, to get rid of a persistent ex or to get rid of debt) should be done on a waning moon, while attraction spells should be done on a waxing moon. So they may feel comfortable doing all energetic cleansing on a waning moon. However, because the spells that you will create here work on the energy matrix that we all operate on in our daily lives, there is no need to wait for a waning moon to begin your energy cleansing routine. The word "routine" is the most important here as you will need to put in a regular time to do this energy cleansing. The frequency of your cleansing will depend on how often you intend to work a magic spell. I would recommend that when you start, you only do one a month so that you can build up your power before you do more frequent ones. As such, a monthly cleanse is most effective.

SALTS LIST

SEA SALT—general use

This is a good choice for both salt baths and salt space clearing. It has the greatest link to the water element and so is good for returning to emotional balance. Particularly good when clearing a room after a fight or other tense occurrence.

TABLE SALT—general use

This is the most processed variety of salt you can get; however, it is cheap and widely available. It is good for use in larger rooms and in emergencies. It is a little harsh on the skin so only use in salt baths if you have nothing else available.

HIMALAYAN SALT—attracting love and good relationships

Since this salt is a lovely pale pink color, it is handy for use in rituals for creating love spells and for those promoting good relationships. It also has a higher iron content making it good for protecting against malevolent influences.

BLACK SALT—personal protection

There are a number of black salts:

WITCH'S SALT—made by mixing the scrapings from the bottom of your ritual cauldron or cast-iron pot, relevant herbs and salt. This is not edible but is great for getting rid of any negative energy around you. Carrying a pouch of this is a good all-round protection.

KALA NAMAK—a sulfurous-smelling salt used in cooking and in Ayurveda in the Indian sub-continent, this is handy in edible spells and charms, and can be ingested.

HAWAIIAN LAVA SALT—made with sea salt and volcanic charcoal, this salt most purely represents the union of all four elements and is a powerful salt to use in personal protection rituals.

OTHER PEOPLE

While other people can be a huge aid to magical work—for example, if you decide to work in a magical partnership or within a coven—they can also occasionally be a hindrance. For example, your partner might protest about the smell of burning herbs or your children might interrupt you when you're in the midst of a cleansing. It might be difficult to find the right time to engage in energetic work but, just as we find the time to physically clean ourselves and our homes, we have to find the time to clear out our energy. You may find you only have time to do a visualization for yourself – this is still better than nothing. Even 5 minutes a day spent in such a meditative state, visualizing yourself bathed in a golden, cleansing light will help you begin your magical work.

If you live with others, you can try to bring your family or housemates into your confidence about your magical work. If you feel it would lead to too much tension, perhaps find your own space in your study or in the garden shed where you won't be disturbed and can do your spellwork in peace. The ideal situation would be to share with your loved ones what you are doing, but not everyone is receptive to magic so use your own judgment.

ENERGY BODIES

Imagine a bird. You can see it in your mind's eye. It has glossy black feathers that are almost blue when the sun hits its wings. The fact that the bird is alive means it is not just that body that you see. If you were able to look at it through "spirit" eyes, you'd see that the bird had an aura around it of various colors. The physical body is the most dense body all living things have. Beyond that there are sheaths of energy that protect the entity and others that project out into the world and draw experiences in. That bird shares this energetic make-up with you as a sentient being. These more subtle bodies are why you sometimes take an instant liking to someone or, conversely, an instant dislike. Our energy bodies are always communicating with others around us and with the energy of a place too. Some places resonate beautifully with us while others feel cold or unwelcoming. Start to become aware of what the energy around people feels like and not just how they look.

THE AURA'S SHEATHS

You have something called an aura surrounding you. This is comprised of subtle energy bodies that make where you end, and the world begins, larger than the boundary of your skin. Different spiritual traditions such as Theosophy, Tantra and Sufism, for example, have different ideas of how those bodies and your aura are ordered and how it all works. Many use the theosophical seven-layer system for ordering the aura. However, for the purposes of this book, we will simply look at two elements of your energy makeup.

Within your aura, at its most outward extent, is the karmic sheath in which you hold a record of all that you've said and done and believed across each of your lives. Karma is the experiences we have over many lives. As corporeal beings, in each life, we take on a variety of different roles and behaviors in order to gain the fullest experience of our corporeality. All of these are then stored in our auras as a permanent record that we carry with us until we fully finish with manifest reality and return to the creation energy from which we were formed at the start of time.

This is not 'cleansed' when you clear your aura. It is the essence of your spirit and requires no cleaning or expunging. What we are actually cleaning is not the part of the aura that remains after our deaths, but the protective sheath, which represents the energy of our current day to day life. This is not permanent and changes moment by moment. It is the energy layer closest to our physical bodies. It is affected by everything from our hormones and moods to external events and our beliefs about ourselves and others. This sheath is also the seat of our intuition and so if it is not strong and well-cleared of problematic influences, it can affect our ability to judge the world around us. It can also leave us open to psychic attack when our beliefs make it porous and susceptible to forming outside circuits.

HOW TO CLEANSE YOUR PROTECTIVE SHEATH

The easiest and most convenient way to cleanse your protective sheath is with visualization. While you can do this practice anywhere – and indeed I'd encourage you to do this on your morning commute if you have one – it is best done initially at a time and place where you will not be disturbed. Take three deep breaths in and out of your nose. You can either close your eyes or, when you become better at visualizing despite visual stimuli, you can do this with your eyes open. Imagine a shaft of white light coming down from the sky (or roof if you're indoors) and entering into the top of your head. As it moves down into the top of your head, it overspills around your entire body. This white light clears all muddiness or stains in your protective sheath and brightens your whole energy outline. It is also under your feet and encompasses the top of your feet and your front and back. You can breathe into this field of energy and in fact it feels clearer, as though the air around you is cleaner and fresher.

Once you have that visualization clear in your mind, seal it as if it is a bubble you are within. Give thanks to whichever deity or simply universal energy for helping you in this way. Then go about your day, knowing you have strengthened your protective sheath.

OTHER WAYS TO PROTECT THIS SHEATH:

✳ Keep a diary of emotions and note who you've seen or spoken to when you feel bad about yourself or in general – always do the visualization whenever you're about to see that person or when you've come from meeting with them.

✳ Always take a salt bath after a fight or confrontation – whether in real life, in your family or online. You can see the different types of salt on page XX – just add a couple of generous handfuls to a warm bath and remember to either submerge the crown of your head or cup your hands and pass the salt water over your head. Shower and moisturize afterwards so that you don't dry out your skin with the salt.

✳ You can also do an egg ritual to cleanse the protective sheath. Take a free-range, organic egg and gently roll it from the top of your head over the whole length of your body. Rub it around your belly and across your genitals. Then crack the egg into the toilet and flush away, visualizing all the 'dirt' in your protective sheath as having been transferred to the egg and flushed away.

STOMACH SHIELD

In terms of your energy make-up, your stomach is the most vital organ. I call this point of energy 'naf', which is the Persian word for belly button. The English word navel comes from an old Anglo-Saxon word *nafela*. The Greek word for navel is *bembix* which literally means whirlpool, hinting at the way that the movement of chakras has been described by almost all energetic medicine practitioners. Most interestingly of all, the root word for umbilical in Latin is *umbo*, which means the boss of a shield—the rounded, strongest part of a shield.

Have you ever said 'I don't have the stomach for it'? This means that you are repelled by an action: you fear it. Queen Elizabeth I of England said,' I know I have the body of a weak and feeble woman, but I have the heart and stomach of a king.' This is a good indication of how far our strength lies in this part of our bodies.

In several cultures around the world, the belly button was closely associated with sex and fertility. This was because the belly button was thought to resemble the vagina. This historical association led to much modern censoring in popular culture of the female navel.

Indian soothsayers believe that a woman with a deep belly button will be much loved by her husband. Thankfully, shallow belly buttons were also good news as they indicated a woman who was generally lucky.

It is not just the human body that has this center of energy: many believe there are places on the earth that serve the same function in physical geography. In Abrahamic religions, Jerusalem is considered the navel of the world. Cuzco, the important city in Peru, is named for the Quechua (Incan) word for navel. The axis mundi (or center of the earth) is said to be the place of connection between heaven and earth. For the Sioux that is the black hills in the Great Plains of North America. Likewise, Mount Fuji is the axis mundi of Japan. Many such centers exist worldwide.

The term 'navel-gazing' is often used in a derogatory way to suggest someone far too interested in themselves or one issue to look up and see the wider picture. However, it actually derives from a spiritual practice common in both ancient Greek and Indian cultures. The Greeks called this *Omphaloskepsis*, a contemplation of the navel that was used as an aid to meditation and communion with divinity. Yogis also undertake this practice and activate the Manipura or nabhi chakra (energy center) to gain insight into the nature of the universe. This chakra center has, in the western alternative spiritual tradition, been associated with power and purpose. It is considered the seat of will. However, other commentators have attributed it with even greater powers.

Swami Brahmavidya, writing in *The Science of Self Knowledge* (1922), revealed the ultimate importance of this energy center for protection work: 'Another great key I will give you is to be found by the contemplation of the Manipur Lotus, which is in the navel, or thereabouts. By contemplating this center, you will be able to enter and go into another person's body, and to take possession of that person's mind, and to cause him to think and to do what you want him to do; you will obtain the power of transmuting metals, of healing the sick and afflicted, and of seership.' These are heady claims indeed, but since we're not up for the unethical controlling of others, we will concentrate on protecting our own naf so that no-one can possess us or deplete our energies.

HOW TO PROTECT YOURSELF

The first principle is to keep your belly button physically clean so get rid of that fluff! Then you should anoint it once a week with consecrated oil. Take a dish of olive or coconut oil and blow into it three times saying aloud each time 'I bless you'. You can add any deity invocation that is appropriate for your particular practice or beliefs. Then, using the middle finger (this is the digit associated with Saturn) of your right hand, dip your finger into the oil and rub it into your belly button in a clockwise direction.

If you are feeling energetically assaulted and are unable to sit and do a ritual with oil, you can also visualize a golden light entering at the top of your head and then coming out of your belly button to form a large, sparkling shield that covers all of your midriff. This will help stop any energetic assaults or vampirism you might come across. Always remember to thank universal energy or the deity you worship when undertaking these visualizations.

OTHER WAYS TO PROTECT YOUR AURA

✂ You can draw the most appropriate charm on a piece of paper, burn it in the fireproof bowl you use for ritual purposes, and apply the ash around your belly button for protection.

✂ Wearing silk is an easy way to protect it, worn as a cumberband or camisole inside your everyday clothes. If you are vegan and not able to wear silk, try the ash or oil anointments as above.

✂ Place your hand at your belly button any time you feel that you're in the company of those who wish you harm. It will provide a measure of comfort and will calm your fear. It will also signal energetically that you are closed off to psychic attack.

HOW TO WORK WITH ENERGY SAFELY

Whenever I give talks on witchcraft, I am always asked about curses and how to protect against them. I explain that it is extremely rare to be the recipient of a curse unless you have agreed on some level to be receptive to it. This is because a curse is like an electrical circuit – it needs unimpeded flow in order to work. If you block or break it, it is impossible for it to work. You leave yourself open to it by expecting that this is what is happening to you. Many get upset when they hear this, thinking that I am blaming them for their own misfortune. This is to miss what I'm saying. We are powerful beings, but we can leave ourselves open to negativity by allowing it into our lives through not maintaining good thinking or energy practices.

Here are some things you can do to ensure you repel negative energy or 'curses':

▷ Do not dwell on the idea of curses or cursing;

▷ Try to think well of people – even those you dislike;

▷ Regularly do the practices in the next section on energy clearing (pages 26-39).

You should also stay intuitively alert. There are times I won't take a certain route home from work, even in broad daylight, simply because I have a feeling I shouldn't. I always discover a reason for why I did not do this such as an act of violence or a disruption of some kind. I am not able to predict what it will be, but I do listen whenever I am told energetically to be elsewhere.

Quite apart from the problems that other people might pose in the form of curses or physical attacks, you yourself are a source of danger if you don't understand the energy work you are doing.

I once visited a woman who ran a goddess group and in her kitchen she had a huge mirror on one wall that was etched with the Sri Yantra. This is a mystical design that represents the union between male and female divinity – the god Shiv and the goddess Shakti. It has many layers of meaning and is one of the most powerful yantras used in the Indian tantric traditions. To put it on a mirror was a terrible idea since this creates a portal through which any number of entities and energies are welcome to enter. I used mudras (hand gestures) to protect myself while in that space, but I didn't leave. The mudras only had a small effect and I was then horribly ill for about six weeks. A lot of my illness was from my own fears regarding the yantra on a mirror. I knew from my knowledge of these powerful diagrams that this was a bad idea, but I allowed the fear of it having a negative effect to become a self-fulfilling prophecy.

Often, when you are working with energy – especially in meditation – you may find yourself feeling light-headed and you might even end up having flu-like symptoms. This is due to a lack of grounding. Before and after any energy work, we need to ensure we ground ourselves back into the real world. The way you can do this very simply is by putting your hands palm-down on the top of your thighs and keeping them there for a few moments. As I mentioned before, we are almost like circuits so whenever you do anything with your palms exposed, energy moves through and out of them. If you want to break the circuit and ground yourself, cutting off the flow from out your palms is a good way to go.

You should also always ensure that any sitting meditations you do are with your feet flat on the ground. Avoid lying down meditations until you are more comfortable with energy work.

PRINCIPLES OF REPELLING AND ATTRACTING

Have you ever had a day when everything just went right? Your commute was great, every decision you made just felt right, and you had oodles of good luck at every turn. Wouldn't it be terrific to have that sort of day on tap all the time? Well, you can.

We all have the ability to bring good things into our lives and to avoid the bad. There are a number of practical actions you can take to ensure you are in the right mindset for attracting the good and repelling the bad. Just be aware that even if it is a mental process, that makes it no less practical and useful. Thoughts are real things and manifest as real allies or obstacles in your life.

GRATITUDE

You will probably have heard how important it is to express gratitude in order to manifest better outcomes in philosophies such as the Law of Attraction. If you regularly give thanks for the blessings in your life, you will find those blessings increase. However, it is also important in order to strengthen your protective sheath. Lack of gratitude or constant complaining can cause fissures and gaps in that protective energy layer and manifest as inflammation in the body that can cause illnesses or mental distress. Certainly I'm sure we can all attest to feeling better when we've spent time in the company of someone who makes you laugh rather than someone who drones on and on about all the terrible things that have happened to them or is likely to happen to them. Of course, we should have compassion for people as we can't always have a joyful experience of life, but if you find that you are also looping into complaint rather than gratitude, make a shift and remind yourself of everything that is great in your life.

POSITIVE THOUGHTS

Thought forms are also important to retaining a clear channel of manifesting the good and repelling the bad. If you find yourself having negative thoughts about any aspect of your day, say to yourself 'I cancel this thought. I am having a great day'. All magic works on the power of belief—some have a greater trust in their ability to manifest than others. Be like them and retain a strong sense of faith made real through good, positive thoughts. Here is an example; have you ever been in an office where everyone does that good-natured eyeroll about how great it is when Friday rolls around? You must not engage with this seemingly harmless group mentality. If you do, you will be telling yourself that you hate your job enough to want Friday to come around. Wouldn't you rather love your job so much that you forget entirely what day it is? Wouldn't it be great not to have the Sunday evening blues? Well, watch your thoughts and your words to avoid those unthinking cues of unhappiness and you'll soon be on your way to attracting the most incredible experience of daily life.

GUT HEALTH

Finally, the naf is also important in this work as you will know 'in your gut' if a particular outcome is right for you. Theodore Zeldin in his classic book An Intimate History of Humanity writes:

'It used to be believed that the stomach was the seat of the emotions, but what actually happens in the stomach when fear is felt – and one vomits, or has butterflies, or has any of the many disabling sensations that the stomach can produce – only became clear in the 1950s.' He gives us the example of a Professor Stewart Wolf of Oklahoma who, over several years, studied Tom, a hospital worker who had burned his oesophagus as a child and could only ingest food through a hole in his stomach. Wolf found that 'the stomach revealed itself as far more interesting than the heart, the supposed seat of emotion, whose monotonous pumping has nothing particularly human about it.'

Wolf could see waterfalls of acid when Tom was fearful and anxiety would turn his stomach pale. The stomach even bled and attempted to destroy its own lining when it felt Tom's circumstances were too hard to bear.

If all energy can be split into love or fear (as many spiritual teachers say) then appeasement of the stomach must feature large in your work – you must take it from fear into love. Attune yourself to the workings of your stomach. Good digestion, perhaps with the aid of the right probiotics and prebiotics if suitable for you personally, must be a key component of your preparation for energy work.

ENERGY CLEARING

KEEPING YOUR PERSONAL ENERGY CLEAR

In the last section we looked at some elements of how to cleanse your energy, protect yourself from psychic attack and attract good things to you. Here we look at how to keep your energy clear on a daily basis in order to create powerful charms and protect yourself from psychic attack.

The greatest, and most difficult, act you can perform for your energetic ablutions is to check your thoughts. You can have as many cleansing ritual baths as you like, but if your thoughts are not monitored to avoid 'ill-speaking' then it will have no effect. You must re-frame your thoughts into higher ones.

For example, you may feel annoyed about someone barging past you on the street. Your impulse might be to quicken to anger, call the person names in your head (or out loud!) and you will feel the adrenaline coursing through your veins as you signal to your brain that you are about to have a row with someone. That 'fight or flight' instinct kicks in almost without you consciously becoming aware of it.

This is problematic for the work we wish to do in this book. This is because whenever you react in that way, you form an energetic link with the object or situation with which you are unhappy. It results in you attracting more of those sorts of unwanted interactions. Think of it as a type of spider web you throw out to the person or situation you hate. Rather than sticking them fast and then ensuring that you can't unstick yourself from them, your thoughts have ensured you are tied until you cut that cord.

The best way to weaken those ties is to immediately recognize when you are going into this scenario. Immediately and consciously think up a reason born out of compassion for the person who has upset you. "Perhaps this person is in a huge rush or has troubles in their life that make them insensible to what they're doing. Perhaps they have been treated discourteously all their lives and only know how to behave discourteously as a result. I bless them on their path and wish them a better journey ahead." Smile as you extend this blessing and it will enrich you as well as the person you are having good thoughts about. The Hawaiian shamanic practitioner, Serge Kahili King, said in a workshop once that when you criticize anything, you create a layer of tension that has an effect on your mind and tenses your body. As such, say true things about what you like rather than speak on what you dislike.

This regular change in your default thoughts will prevent negative cords forming, but you can also dissolve or cut them through your own energy clearing.

CORD CUTTING

It is not just negative cords that are linked in to you; each and every interaction creates a cord. Our strongest cord is the link to our biological mother. Even if you never knew your mother, your mother was abusive or your mother has died, the link remains a primary one. This is not because of who your human mother is, it is because this cord is the one that is the birth cord – the interaction that made you manifest from divine energy, it is representative of the divine 'mother', the source of all creation. When we speak of cord cutting, you cannot sever this cord, but you can certainly sever any negative ones that are connecting you to your human mother.

- ✄ Right before you take any of the baths in the next section, stand naked in front of a mirror. If you don't have a mirror in a room that you can stand naked in or you don't have a mirror large enough, don't worry. Just stand up straight with nothing around you and your feet firmly planted on the floor.

- ✄ Half close your eyes until your sight is slightly blurred.

- ✄ Using your right hand, take the flat of your hand and pass it over your body, starting at the crown and slowly going over each bit of your body. Don't touch your body, just pass your hand close to your body as if you were stroking your protective sheath.

- ✄ Try and feel for where the energy feels 'sticky' or otherwise denser. It may be that you feel this at your throat. This is very common for people who don't know what to say when they are being verbally attacked and can only think up an appropriate response after the moment has passed.

- ✄ When you get to such a place, scoop the energy up with your hand and throw it away from your body. This is just like you would if you walked into a cobweb and were removing it from your body. You may even 'feel' strands like hairs when you are doing this.

- ✄ After doing this, immediately have one of the baths in the next section.

RITUAL BATHING

Bathing has been proven to be great for the circulation and to enable a good night's sleep due to the changes in your body temperature when you emerge from a hot bath. The Japanese have a bath ritual called *ofaru*, often done collectively at a public bathhouse called an *onsen*. The Romans also elevated bathing to a ritual art, building beautiful aqueducts near healing springs to enable bathers to take the waters.

Santeria, the African-Caribbean tradition that developed from the Yoruba West African religion in Cuba, also relies heavily on a ritual bathing practice. Santeria is a Spanish word meaning 'worship of the saints'. Santeria was developed in order to hide worship of the Orishas (deities and human embodiments of the spirits) behind western Saints in the Roman Catholic religion. Important within the tradition is the connection with the Egun (ancestors).

Here are a couple of baths that help with clearing your personal energy and appealing to your Egun for help and guidance.

The Queen's Bath

This is a bath primarily for women, particularly those suffering from a lack of self-esteem or those regularly attracting unhappy circumstances such as bad relationships or difficult living situations.

Ingredients:

▷ A cup of goat's milk
▷ White or yellow gold flowers (no roses)
▷ Florida water (you can get this online or in any store selling Caribbean or Latin American products – use the amount that feels right to you)
▷ Honey
▷ 2 coconuts

Run a hot bath. Pour all the ingredients, save the honey or the water from one of the coconuts, into the bath. Do this with intent, knowing that you are asking your ancestors to bless the water that you are about to get into. Then crack the second coconut (I keep a hammer for cracking open coconuts – it is more potent than just buying coconut water as its energy is contained in the nut) and standing on a towel, pour the water over your head. Take the honey and rub it all over your body, concentrating on the belly and navel. Then get into the bath and soak, imagining that all psychic 'dirt' is coming away in the water and all the good energy of the honey, flowers and perfumed water is entering your body. You can shower as normal afterwards. Thank your ancestors before you go to sleep that night.

LUCK BATH

This is suitable for both men and women and it removes bad luck as well as strengthening your power. Have this bath early on a day that you don't mind having flowers and leaves dried upon you since you do not wash or brush off any remnants of this particular bath until the next day.

Ingredients:

▹ Bunch of finely chopped basil
▹ Bunch of finely chopped parsley
▹ Petals from a bunch of flowers (avoid roses)
▹ Florida water
▹ Small bottle of whiskey
▹ Pinch of tobacco

Mix the ingredients in a bowl and leave overnight covered with a white muslin cloth. In the morning, run a hot bath and sitting in that bath, ritually pour the bowl of bath ingredients over your head. It will feel cold, but you should feel fine about it since you are sat in a hot bath.

Do not submerge your head and resist the urge to wipe away any leaves left stuck to you. Sit close-eyed in the bath for a while thinking about what you would like to manifest in your life and the ways in which you seek protection from the spirits and your ancestors. If your belief system does not allow for spirits, deities or ancestor guides, you can express gratitude to the secular universal energy that comprises us and all things. You should leave the flowers and leaves to dry on you naturally, only washing them off the next morning.

(Practical tip: get yourself a strainer for the bath drain to avoid leaves and flower petals blocking your pipes. Despite the sacred and ritual nature of these baths, you can put any waste leaves and petals in your compost or usual disposal.)

NB: roses are avoided because they have a special energy that, while used in some workings, are not compatible with the baths given here.

CREATING SPACE FOR ENERGY WORK

Your home is where you will create your charms and it needs to be able to support energy work. This means that you should have a clear, calm space in which to make your charms. It goes without saying that clutter is not helpful when it comes to energy work; this is not because it isn't pretty to look at, but because of the guilt you feel when you look at something you have yet to deal with. Clutter is essentially decisions you aren't making so the first thing you have to do is trust yourself to make decisions regarding your stuff. This will support your trust in your own abilities to create the life you want.

Don't handle anything more than once and don't put it down until you have decided precisely what to do with – find it a home, put it in a bag to go to the charity shop or throw it away if it is broken. Don't get waylaid with "I might need this" or "I could fix this" – you could, but to date you haven't. So either fix it immediately or put it in an appropriate place and diarise exactly when you'll have the time and tools to fix it or let it go. You need to trust yourself and not let fear-based clutter take over your space.

Once you are rid of your clutter, you should also do a top to bottom clean of your home – or, at the very least, the room in which you intend to craft your charms. Get help if you can't manage it yourself or even hire a cleaner to do a one-off clean if you can afford it. Try and use ecologically sound cleaning materials as you want to ensure that you are keeping the planet as clean and healthy as you want your home to be. A lot of old cleaning solutions are natural and only require elbow grease.

You may then look around at your tidy and clean room and think that this is it. It is not. Everything is energetically charged as well. Cleaning and tidying begin to shift up the energetic dust, but it doesn't clean it up so you can have a perfectly clean and tidy space that is energetically filthy because it is the scene of trauma or of repressed rage and negative emotion.

There are several ways you can clear a space energetically. For example, you can:

🌿 smudge a room by passing appropriate burning herbs or spices through it – sage is traditionally used for this purpose but you can also use rosemary, basil or cloves

🌿 scatter sea salt over the carpet, ensuring you go into corners, leaving it for an hour or two, and then vacuuming it up

🌿 place a bowl of filtered water in each corner of the room, blow into each bowl while holding the intent to energetically clear the room into the water, leave for an hour, and then pour away the water into your lawn or a drain or running water

🌿 you can also clear a room with sound using either chanting, drumming or even a handclap in each corner of the room as long as you visualize the sound-waves cleaning out the room's energy.

ENERGETIC RITUALS

You should feel a shift in your energy and the energy of the room that you practice in when you have finished the clearing as per the instructions on pages 26-33, irrespective of which methods you use. However, it important to maintain that feeling in order for your charms to be effective. Here are some rituals and routines that will help you do so.

DAILY

MORNING ROUTINE

▷ During your morning teeth brushing and face washing, take water in your right palm and touch it three times to the top of your head saying each time 'may divinity flow through me today'.

▷ Then do the same to the point of your third eye, between your eyebrows, three times saying 'may I see clearly today'.

▷ Then do so at your throat, again three times, saying at each splash, 'may I speak well of all today'.

▷ In the shower, take water in your right hand and hold it over your chest, saying 'may love flow through me today'. You do not splash at this lower energy centers as the energy here is of a different movement.

▷ Then at your belly button, take water into your right hand and hold it there 'may the divine protect me from harm today'.

▷ Then at the point halfway between your belly button and your genitals, take water in your right hand and hold it there saying 'may I choose love over fear'.

▷ Finally, wash at the point of your perineum (between your genitals and your anus) saying 'may I be rooted in the strength and power of my ancestors and spirit guides'.

This daily morning bathing ritual will keep your energy up all day long and help on days where things aren't quite right.

Evening routine

▷ Have a 15 minute tidy up of your house when you get in from work. Your instinct will be to plop and relax on the sofa as soon as you get in, but while the kettle is boiling or the wine is breathing, have a very quick zoom around and ensure everything is back where it should be.

▷ Tune in to the energy of your home at the end of the day – does anywhere feel particularly disturbed? Do you feel cold in a spot of your house? Or have any sense of general unease in a particular room? Smudge it to ensure that the energy stays clear.

▷ Before you go to bed, thank your body for sustaining you throughout the day. We can have a lot of negative self-talk about our bodies, but they are miraculous vehicles to which we should be very grateful. In bed, do the same for your house. A roof over your head is a blessing many don't enjoy so express gratitude to the home that holds you each night.

This simple evening routine will help ground you in your home and make it a haven for you. If you have time and want to do so, you can also have a specific time (perhaps half an hour before bed) at which you lower the lights, light some perfumed candles or incense and change into more comfortable clothes. Having a routine for relaxing at home is a great boon for energy work.

WEEKLY

1. Once a week, you should do a house blessing through the medium of sweeping. Using the besom or natural broom that we mentioned at the start of this section, sweep your rooms, moving everything toward the door out of the room and eventually sweep the dust and dirt over your threshold, out the front or back door. You can sweep it up once it is past your threshold. Then do the practical step of vacuuming. You will have disturbed any stagnant energy with the intentional sweeping and the vacuuming is simply to clean the space.

2. Once this is done, wash out a clean, lint-free cloth and put a couple of drops of essential oils on it (choose the one that appeals to you the most or decide from the correspondences opposite). Wipe all your skirting boards and surfaces that are able to be touched with oil. As you go, imagine a golden sheen is appearing on those surfaces and sealing them.

3. Water your plants as necessary, having a little chat with them if you're so inclined. This is also the time to remove any dead leaves or do any trimming, if the season is right.

4. Finally, after your weekly clean is over (and bear in mind the routines above are in addition to whatever your usual cleaning regime is), brew a cup of tea.

ESSENTIAL OIL CORRESPONDENCES

Basil – to enhance wealth

Bergamot – to stimulate energy

Jasmine – to cure insomnia, remember happy memories

Orange – also good for physical energy and cheerfulness

Eucalyptus – releases negative energy from fights

Lavender – aids good sleep and
encourages good-naturedness

Clary sage – destresses and helps acceptance

Ylang Ylang – promotes romantic
love and enhances sexuality

You can find many different oil blends out there –
speak to an aromatherapist and see if they can create
a blend that works best for you on all levels.

MONTHLY

Party time! Once a month, hold a party to honor the energies that help you and elevate your energy to a higher plane. There is no point doing all this energy work to protect yourself when there is no joy in the doing of it or no reminding yourself of what the whole point of living is. So, once a month, throw a party – even if just for yourself.

Now, when we think of parties, we think of expense and invites and loud music and overall organizational hassle. This is not what I mean here. You are changing the energy of your home by inviting others into it. That can be for a very sedate, sophisticated tea party with only two other friends or it can be an elaborate masked ball. It can even be a night that you put aside to celebrate with your spirits and ancestors alone with good food and drink and a movie that reminds you of the world beyond the mundane. The important thing is the feeling that the night gives you. The anticipation beforehand, the joy of the actual night, and the feeling of satisfaction you get afterwards as you clean up and remember all the funny things said and done in the night.

If you can't entertain at home for any reason, it also fine to go out and see others for you carry your energy with you all the time and will bring back that elevated feeling when you return. You could arrange to meet at a new bar or restaurant. If you do, pay attention to the whole night from what people are wearing to the décor of the place to the drinks consumed. Turn up with all your attention and keep your mobile phone in your bag so that you engage directly and openly with your friends in real life.

Just remember though, if your intuition tells you not to go out – because you're coming down with an illness or you're not up for company that night – there is no shame in canceling or rescheduling. True friends understand when we're not able to meet a commitment.

However, if this happens to you a lot, do think about why in your next meditation. Ask your ancestors or guides or subconscious to reveal why you always feel the need to cancel. Are you afraid of something? Perhaps even afraid of having a good time and leaving your unhappiness behind? Sometimes people are so afraid that everyone will think they are okay and stop checking in on them if they are strong, healthy and happy that they retain a vulnerability they could easily lose. Reliability is a good trait to have and if you are finding yourself becoming more unreliable, have a proper conversation with yourself – without judgment or beating yourself up about it – to discover why that might be.

STATE OF BEING

"Tell me what to do! You know all that voodoo hocus-pocus stuff." My friend is beside herself. She is afraid that the father of her child is about to leave her and that she will never be happy. I tell her how to connect with her ancestors and ask some pertinent questions of them as to whether she is even meant to be with this man. "Oh God no, I can't conjure up spirits – that would be like in a horror movie!" Alas all my 'voodoo hocus-pocus stuff' relies on connecting with things beyond solid matter.

In our ancient societies, we knew that there was more to the world than what met the eye. We had a much more friendly relationship with gods, spirits and dead ancestors. We even had a much more friendly relationship with fear. We knew that fear was necessary on occasion to motivate us, it was the companion to our rites of passage, the bedfellow to our big life milestones. We knew fear to be natural and, pardon the paradox, that it was nothing to be afraid of. Now, we avoid it at all costs.

When you begin energy work, there will be miracles and coincidences that will leave you in shock and awe. Sudden windfalls of money that are precisely what you asked for down to the last penny. A weird connection between two parts of your life you were never aware of that suddenly bring you the opportunity you had been praying for. And, on occasion, a glimpse into parallel worlds and spirit worlds.

If you are interested in understanding the true nature of the magical being that you are, by your very birthright, you have to get used to that sort of thing. My friend was not ready for that and so bumbled along with ordinary advice and eventually worked it out, after a fashion.

Had she been a bit braver, I would have recommended setting up an altar at which she could communicate with her ancestors and/or spirit guides. Whenever you consecrate any flat plane, keep it clean, and put sacred objects upon it, it becomes an altar. It is a place to sit or stand or kneel before and, through the very act of being there, enter into a state of calm meditation. You can place the charms that you will learn about in the next section on this altar or you can keep it clear of anything except a single flame that you light whenever you want to enter into that state of communion. Some people, if they follow a particular religion or tradition, will have an icon or image that reminds them of the deity that they worship. You put whatever turns your mind to the spirit world outside normal experience on this surface.

If you have a spare bedroom in which you can set up this altar, all the better, as then you can keep this room for your energy work such as meditation and crafting charms. Bedrooms are good for this purpose as it should be a space that brings you a sense of rest and relaxation. Try and keep electrical devices out of this room so that you enter a state of focus when you go in there. If you don't have a spare room, a corner of any of your rooms is do-able, just don't put it up in a high traffic area where you will constantly be disturbed.

Once you have set up your altar, light the candle and sit or stand before it for a while, steadying your breathing and letting your focus in your vision soften. Begin by saying 'For the highest good, and with the help of my ancestral spirits, I petition the universal energy to answer my question.' Then, pick a single question that you need guidance on and hold the question in your mind. Phrase it in such a way that it gives you guidance on whether an outcome is right for you rather than whether it will happen. So, in the case above, not "will he leave me?" but "are we right for each other?"

Pay attention to any images, words or ideas that pop into your head when you're asking in the intentional way. They are all clues as to what your spirits are telling you.

Don't keep asking the same question. There is nothing more annoying for those giving advice than to be asked the same thing again and again in the hope of a different answer. It may give you an idea of what YOU'd like to have happen, but that isn't the same as what the spirits or your highest destiny has in mind for you.

NOURISHING YOUR BODY

A really important part of energy work is what goes into your body. When you undertake shamanic work, you often fast beforehand in order to purify the body and enable it to communion with spirits better. In protection work, the denser the body, the better. This is because you are closing down your body to anyone or anything other than the ancestral or divine spirits that you yourself are inviting in for connection and guidance.

I tend to find that people truly love this part of my advice. You should eat what makes you happy. Obviously not to excess, because that might cause you other bodily problems, but it should be what makes your toes curl with pleasure. Once you have properly honored and connected with your own energy, you will find that you know precisely what you need to feel good. Sometimes your body will crave salt because it needs it. At other times, sweet things or vegetables or meat. Listen to its needs and don't do faddy diets. Eat less of the thing you're craving if you feel that it will cause you to put on unwanted weight, but don't deny yourself it in the name of any diet program.

You will find that historically a number of occultists were traditionally bigger than average. This is because the density of the body aids in providing another layer of energy for anything intrusive to have to get through before the protective sheath or the naf was reached.

If you ever work with teaching plants, you will follow a very bland diet before having the ceremony. This is to make your body a comfortable home for the teacher plant. However, if you're not communing with a plant spirit, it is grounding to eat meat, spices and salt.

Ethically our farming systems are indefensible, but more and more higher welfare meat is available in our stores and you should choose that, even if more expensive. Eat less, but eat more ethically. If you're a vegan, choose mushrooms and potatoes as foods to ground yourself. If you can bake, make your own bread – this is a very good way to nourish yourself and your family. Think about the safety, health and happiness of you and yours while you knead the bread and you will produce a loaf that is not just a foodstuff but is a magical spell of protection for everyone who eats it.

EVERYDAY COMFORT

You know that feeling you get when you get in freshly bathed into a bed made with fresh linen and the scent of night-time essential oil blend is in the room? It is that level of "aah" comfort that you are aiming for in this section.

Why is this important? The reason is that if you embrace everyday comfort, anything that is energetically or physically uncomfortable will stick out like a sore thumb. You will recognize it far more easily if you've become accustomed to everyday comfort. Not only that, but it is a good way to live and honor your corporeal existence.

I recall once house-sitting for a friend whose house was the most infuriating place I have ever stayed in. If you went to get something out of a drawer, the drawer felt apart or stuck. There were odd, heavy bits of furniture blocking your path and ensuring you always stubbed a toe or hit a shin walking past. His kitchen had a broken window with cardboard blocking it that was a) a safety hazard, b) a security hazard and c) made standing there doing the dishes very cold. Finally, his plumbing left much to be desired with the water pressure in the bathroom very low and the heating erratic. This left me very confused as my friend had enough money and sense to take care of all these things. When I asked why he hadn't fixed it all, he said that he had called a plumber, a carpenter, and a window repair person but nobody had turned up when he booked them. Three tradespeople – all unreliable?!? That didn't seem creditable to me and so I started calling around for him while he was away.

The first day, his assessment was correct – people either didn't answer or didn't turn up when they said they would. So then, knowing what I know about energy, I took out the worst of his drawers – from a dresser in the bedroom – and taking a hammer and some nails, I fixed that drawer. I sanded the bottom of it as well so that when it went back in the dresser, it now slid open easily and closed gently. The carpenter called me back that afternoon and arranged to come and do the other small fixes in the house. I then tided away any loose glass from the window and removed the cardboard from it.

I prepared it as though a glazier were due to come that day and called the mobile of the company again. I got through immediately and a very helpful man came by an hour later and fixed the window. I didn't even need to do anything with the water or heating because the plumber came by with huge apologies for not having turned up the day before. In the space of two days, the greatest of his house fixes were done. I then – with his permission – re-arranged his furniture and made the energy flow better in his house. The whole feel of the place immediately changed and it was no longer a house at war with its occupant. My friend lived there very comfortably and happily for several years.

What happened in that example above is that I committed to fixing the things that were wrong and the universe conspired to help me. When you make a decision to get your energetic house in order, the universe or divine energy or luck will be on your side. However, you must make that commitment first and one of the easiest, most enjoyable ways you can do so is to keep an eye open for your comfort at all times.

Treat yourself like a most beloved friend who is staying with you. Ask yourself the following questions.

THE FRIEND TEST

▷ What would you do if your friend was wearing painful shoes or uncomfortable clothes? Would you offer her insoles, suggest she buy new shoes, let her change into a more comfy t-shirt from your wardrobe?

▷ If your pal was coming around, would you be happy with her seeing your house as it is right now? Is it clean? Is it comfortable?

▷ What sort of food and drink you would serve her? Would you serve it on a nice dish or out of the carton?

Everyday comfort involves treating yourself well and if it takes you thinking about how you'd treat others that you respect in order to treat yourself the same way, then use that as a prop to get yourself in the right mindset.

ENERGY DETECTiNG

Once you're in the mindset of creating everyday comfort for yourself, you can also go through your house and detect places of stuck energy or tension. The way to do this is to notice when you're next frustrated by some element of your living space.

Do you huff when you realize that you have to go back upstairs to the bedroom to get the nice bath salts because you forgot to take them in with you when you took your towel and clothes into the bathroom? Find a place either in or near the bathroom to keep the salts in.

Is your laundry basket at the back of the utility cupboard where none of your family can be bothered to go into to leave their dirty clothes? Buy a prettier basket (or several) and keep them in a place where your family can drop their clothes on their way past.

Keep stepping on kids' toys? Colorful bins around the edge of a room where small hands can drop in their toys with ease will help.

Can you never find your keys? A set of hooks by the front door or a plate in the hallway where you can always hang or drop your keys when you come in will work wonders.

Is your coffee table too large and unwieldy? Sell it and use the money to buy someone more in proportion with your requirements.

Is it someone else's 'stuff' that gets in your way? Tidy your own stuff away first and keep it tidy for a while and you'll soon notice that your arch-ne-mess-is (see what I did there?) also starts putting his or her stuff away.

This is an ongoing investigation so do keep detecting where things can be better utilized. You will find that as you begin the process of making energy flow better in your home, you will suddenly get brilliant ideas for where things can go that will work better.

Once you get to the stage that the energy is flowing well through your home and you are personally also comfortable in your body and what you're wearing, you can begin the process of creating protection charms. You have laid the important foundations on which you can build your magical symbols of security and prosperity.

WORKING INTUITIVELY

2
CRAFTING GOOD SPELLS

Our earliest examples of art show that we had the ability to make symbols that represented outcomes even then. We understood sympathetic magic (that something that looks like a thing might affect that thing). We drew pictures of hunts in which we would be successful before going out on real hunts in the hope that our symbolic etchings might come to pass. We drew vaginas and phalluses in the hope of fertility and children borne out of that fecundity. We have carried trinkets in our pockets to ward off ill luck since Neolithic times. Our ancestors believed that there is a kingdom of spirits out there to guard us and all that was needed was to figure out the correct way of contacting them.

As the Abrahamic religions took hold, our belief in the power of charms and amulets did not fall way, in fact, it was taken up by these new religions and incorporated into them. So you get the Jewish Mezuzah (a charm within which prayers are inserted into a container and hung on the wall or around the neck), Christian verbal charms (particularly prevalent in Ireland where sickness was kept at bay with saints' prayers) and Muslim amulets (in which magic squares are made corresponding to Quranic verse numbers and inserted into a square metal locket to be worn around the neck). Making ancient protection charms acceptable to monotheistic religions was done by taking old practices and attributing their workings to the Judeo-Christian-Islamic God.

While our ancestors sought to avoid disease and pestilence with their charms – and in many cases, ever-prevalent early death – we can use the same principles to concentrate our minds on manifesting the things that cause us to feel happier and more secure.

WORKING WITH CHARMS

Sound is an important component in working with charms. Many charms were simply verbal and we can find these worldwide. For example, in the 17th and 18th century Russians were using many verbal charms (*zagovory*) in order to effect the outcome of court cases and influence the Tsar and the royal family. Researcher Andrei L. Toporkov writes:

'The magical purpose of these verbal charms was to have an influence on authorities and judges, to alter the way they felt and their will, their mood and spiritual condition. The tradition of incantations if seen as a whole did not force a person to take this or that specific attitude toward the authorities, but rather offered the possibility of choice either to consider the object of the charm as an implacable foe, deserving of annihilation (if only symbolic), or as someone more positive, from whom love is coaxed.'

These verbal charms were ritualistically incanted before the inciting incident such as a court case. Here is an example of one:

GIVE ME THE HEART OF A LION AND A LARYNX
LIKE THE JAW OF THE PROWLING WOLF. LET
MY OPPONENT, MY RULER [INSERT NAME], HAVE
THE HEART OF HARE, EARS OF A GROUSE AND
EYES LIKE A DEAD MAN'S CORPSE; THAT HE
NOT MANAGE TO OPEN HIS MOUTH AND THAT
HIS CLEAR EYES BE TROUBLED, THAT HE NOT
TO RAIL AGAINST ME IN HIS ZEALOUS HEART,
THAT HIS WHITE HANDS NOT BE RAISED UP
AGAINST ME, SERVANT OF GOD [INSERT NAME].

The charms we will work with here are not verbal charms but are textual charms and physical ones. However, you can imbue them with more power by chanting over them after you have finished making them or receiving them if made by someone else.

A textual charm is written on a piece of paper and either ingested by means of swallowing with water or folded up tiny, put into an amulet necklace, and worn at all times.

In ancient Rome, freeborn boys were given a bulla (amulet) nine days after birth, which would protect the child from evil spirits, and was only removed when the boy came of age. Girls were given another sort of amulet called a lunula, which was worn until the day before her marriage when it was removed along with all the other trappings of childhood.

NATURE'S BOUNTY

Botanicals form a large part of spells and spellcrafting. This is because spellcraft is deeply linked to nature and the world around us. The energy of plants resonates deeply with us and with what we wish to achieve when making a spell. The scent of certain plants transports us to a magical place where we can access a deeper knowing than our everyday awareness. The elements of nature—earth, air, fire, and water—are considered fundamental building blocks in the practice of magic, each offering unique energies and properties that can be harnessed for various spells and rituals.

The earth element represents stability, grounding, and fertility. It is associated with the physical body, financial prosperity, and material aspects of life. Spellcrafters often use herbs, stones, and soil in their rituals to invoke the stabilizing and nurturing energies of the earth. Gardens, forests, and mountains are seen as sacred spaces where one can connect deeply with this element, drawing strength and sustenance from the natural world.

Air symbolizes intellect, communication, and the breath of life. It is linked to the mind, clarity of thought, and the power of the spoken word. Spellcrafters might incorporate feathers, incense, and bells into their practices to channel the airy energies. Open skies, windy plains, and high altitudes are revered as places where the air element is particularly potent, providing a conduit for insight, inspiration, and the dispersal of negative energies.

Fire embodies transformation, passion, and willpower. It is the element of change, destruction, and rebirth. Candles (see pages 62–63), bonfires, and smoldering embers are common tools in fire-based spellcraft, symbolizing the spark of life and the potential for personal transformation. Volcanic landscapes, deserts, and sunny meadows are environments where fire's energy can be strongly felt, offering opportunities for profound inner change and renewed vigor.

Water represents emotion, intuition, and healing. It is connected to the subconscious mind, dreams, and the fluidity of life. Spellcrafters may use seashells, river stones, and water itself in their rituals to invoke the cleansing and transformative properties of this element. Oceans, rivers, and lakes are sacred sites where water's energies are most accessible, providing a space for emotional release, psychic enhancement, and spiritual purification.

Beyond the individual elements, nature as a whole is regarded as a living, breathing entity that is interconnected with all aspects of life. Spellcrafters believe that by attuning themselves to the rhythms of the natural world—such as the cycles of the moon, the changing of the seasons, and the movement of the stars—they can align their own energies with those of the universe. This alignment enhances their ability to manifest intentions, heal themselves and others, and connect with the divine.

Through understanding how nature and the elements inform the magical practice of more seasoned practitioners, you will also be able to craft spells that are powerfully effective. Try to go on magical nature walks as often as you can. Keep your eyes open for signs and symbols that can then be used in your spellwork.

In my local area, we have an abundance of crows, rabbits and foxes. I have received many messages from them, simply by watching their behavior. A rabbit or fox that is bold and doesn't bolt away on your approach may be telling you to stand your ground in a situation where you feel stronger actors are determining your life. Crows are especially helpful in that they are often conduits between the spirit world and the manifest one. I have learned that seeing a crow is often a lucky emblem for me as this is the way that my ancestors communicate with me. You will find your own animal allies and messages from nature, in your own country and region. Just keep those eyes and ears open to what the spirits are trying to tell you.

SEASONAL ALTARS

Alongside the elements, you can also work with the seasons. Spellcrafting requires an intimate connection with nature and the world around you. Being aware of which season you're in and honoring that on your altar is a simple way to show that connection. Even if you live somewhere that doesn't really have seasons in terms of significant weather changes, you can still acknowledge the turning of the year's wheel by marking on your diary the four seasons and changing up what is on your altar at those times. If you live in the Southern Hemisphere then be aware that you should combine not just the weather conditions in your honoring of the seasons, but also your primary culture. So a winter's altar for you might include a fan to represent air in the hot sun and fairy lights to represent the celebration of Saturnalia if your culture is likely to celebrate Christmas at that time. Stay true to what feels right for you.

If you are based in the Northern Hemisphere, you can use some conscious walks to forage for items to place on your altar. From driftwood that comes ashore in winter to spring flowers (ensure you only pick what is legal to pick and abundant in your local area) and summer blooms or fall leaves and seeds, there is plenty of bounty in nature that it is permissible and good to use. You can also add in fruit that is in season. Place on your altar for the full moon night and eat the next day, having shared in the nutritious energy with your ancestors and spirit guides. If you prefer, you can bury the fruit you place in your altar or place it in your garden for animals to enjoy.

Consider doing a ritual four times a year as you change up the items on your altar. This will align you with what you wish to bring in to your magic and spellcrafting. So to attract new relationships or a new job, you can concentrate your efforts in your spring altar as this is the time for renewal, rebirth and new beginnings. To find fertile ground for your desires, a summer altar is a good one to concentrate on. By fall, you are ready for those things you wish to eliminate from your life, whether it is getting rid of bad habits like dead leaves falling from a tree or bad players who are causing you heartache. This is the altar at which you can cut your ties to them. A winter altar is a powerful one on which to lay your plans out for the next turn of the wheel. Like a seed lies dormant in winter and bursts into life in the spring, so must your plans be laid quietly in the dark. It is a time to rest and conserve energy that you may burst forth in the warmth with spells to bring forth all you desire.

PLACES OF POWER

We often enhance our spiritual experience by going on pilgrimages. These may be religious ones or entirely secular ones—for example, if you revisit a house or town you grew up in. As humans our sense of place is deeply embedded in our psyches and when you decide to do magic, you need to be intimately aware of what will impress your spirit enough to communicate your desires clearly to the Universe at large.

Some places exude a powerful presence because people have attributed magical meaning to them. Consider stone circles or deep caves. Whether made by humans or by nature, some places feel different to the workaday energy of our usual dwellings. One of the best ways of enhancing your spellcraft is to connect with your places of power. This can be done in a very practical way, simply by sitting and running through your memories of where you have felt particularly affected by your surroundings. Don't censor yourself because even if you have special feelings for a car park or a storage unit, that is valid to you. Energy doesn't discriminate and where powerful associations have been made, there is magic to be tapped into.

If you are at a loss for your places of power and even visiting the places that most other people consider to be powerful, such as the sea or a woodland glen or other places of that sort, leaves you feeling detached, it may help to this meditative practice.

At a time when you know you won't be disturbed for half an hour or so, sit in a comfortable position with your feet placed flat on the ground and your hands on your lap facing upwards. Close your eyes and take a couple of deep breaths in and out through your nose.

Imagine that there is a pure white light coming down from the sky into the top of your head. As it passes down through your body, feel the warmth of its light making its way through every pore. Allow that light to pool in your upturned palms. As those two balls of light grow bigger in your mind's eye, gently bring your palms together and combine the two balls of light into one larger one. Cup your hands as if you are holding this big ball of light in your hands.

Within that ball, now imagine that you are seeing a path within it. Keep your eyes closed and just visualize as clearly as possible what this path looks like. It may be a wide highway or a small, narrow path in a woodland setting. Walk down this path until you come to a clearing. This clearing is a place of power. You can feel it surging and swirling in and around the space. You might be able to see this as rays or strings of light. Make a note of the color and the shape of what you are seeing. Once you have done that, ask the space to name itself for you.

The way you can do this is simply to ask, even out loud, "what is your name?" and then listen to the answer you receive. You may find that it isn't the name of a specific place, but the name of a type of place, such as "Coast" or "Mountain". This is fine, as you are just beginning your journey and it may take some time to find all the specific places that resonate with you and your energy.

Ensure you keep an eye out for what attracts your attention, whether that is a picture in a magazine or a friend's social media images. If you find that there is something that calls to you, you must make sure you write it down in your Book of Shadows so that you can find a way to get to it in real life. Sometimes you may find that you are attracted to a scene of a place that doesn't exist. Digitally manipulated images or images in a science fiction show or movie. This is fine, it is the spirit of the place that you are evoking rather than a place itself.

CANDLE MAGIC

Since humans discovered the ability to make fire, they have been fascinated by flames. Think of sitting in front of a real log fire and you probably think of words like "cozy" and "romantic". This is because the focus of your eyes softens, your heartbeat seems to slow down and you feel content and full of love and well-being when in front of such a fire. This state of pleasurable warmth and relaxation is what candle magic is all about.

Real magic comes from relaxed but focused intent. You can use the instructions opposite to get started but then begin to think about your own spellcrafting with candles. Get creative! When you are passionate about the mysterious world around you, everything else will fall into place.

Safety note: Candles have a tendency to want to tip over and start dramatic fires. Make sure your candles behave themselves by keeping them away from paper or curtains, and ensuring you don't leave them unattended.

What you will need:

Candles of the correct color for the spell you're doing: three is a good number of candles to have, avoid using an even number of candles in your workings (if you were to divide an even number by two, you're left with nothing and that's not what you want).

> **For love:** red for passion, pink for romance, white for fidelity in love, blue for a wedding
>
> **For money:** green, blue, gold
>
> **For binding (for example to stop an ex from hounding you):** white, black
>
> **For spiritual insights:** violet, purple
>
> **For health:** orange, red, yellow, gold, natural beeswax
>
> **For a new home:** gray, green, black

Scented essential oil, mixed in with a base oil like almond. You don't need lots of it as you're just going to be using it to gently anoint your candle with your index finger.

> **For love:** rose, gardenia
>
> **For money:** basil, bergamot
>
> **For binding:** cypress
>
> **For spiritual insights:** frankincense, jasmine
>
> **For health:** tea tree, lavender
>
> **For a new home:** ylang ylang

Take a candle of the appropriate color and anoint with the specified oil, working from base to top. Use a sharp pencil or pin to carve your name from base to top of the candle on one side. On the other side of the candle score it so that you divide it into seven roughly equal parts, leaving the base part as the largest. Then light the candle. Sit in quiet contemplation while the candle burns down. Let it burn to the first score mark. Once it has burnt down to the first notch, blow it out, saying "thank you" to whatever divine power you recognize. For the next six days continue to burn the candle down one more notch each night, always concentrating on the positive elements of what you want to manifest. Once the candle has burnt down to its stub, bury the stub in your garden placing a little food like a sliced apple or something else appropriate on top of where you've buried it for garden wildlife to enjoy.

MAGICAL PROTECTION

When you begin spellcrafting, you may find that you come across a lot of ominous warnings about protecting yourself from magical attack or "curses". This is often given as something that is likely to happen when you begin to work on magic. This is not the case. Generally speaking, as long as you keep your energy clear and work in an ethical way, it is highly unlikely that you will need to worry too much about negative forces.

However, there is no harm in keeping yourself protected with simple practices that you can do without much extra effort. For example, it is simply good practice to keep your altar clean and tidy and to remove any of the ingredients for old spells. Too much build-up of old energy can cause blockages in what you want to manifest now.

In terms of symbols used universally in magical protection, you may see many of them out and about in the world. From an image of the Green Man in someone's garden to the charms a person wears on their wrist, we are all happier when we think there is some extra protection out there for us.

In classical works of the western world, the evil eye was the ability to cause harm through gaze alone that was said to reside in certain individuals. However, in eastern cultures, this ability is acknowledged as being more widely distributed with anyone being able to give you the evil eye through a sudden bout of jealousy or pique. This is why charms are so often deployed to give a more general protection against a cursing look from others – whether intended or not.

You will have seen amulets with a blue and white circle to protect against the evil eye. These can be found on touristy items from countries such as Turkey or Egypt. In the use of such charms, the circles represent an eye that acts like a mirror and reflects the evil eye back to the sender.

Blue is traditionally used as a color for these charms as it used to be believed that light-eyed people, being rare in the countries where belief in the evil eye originates, could give the curse through their gaze. So, in a case of sympathetic magic, the color is used to block the effect.

In making your own charm with this symbol, be aware that it can protect a home, possessions, a person and animals so you can put it on virtually anything you wish to protect.

❀ A writer might have it on the front of a notebook.

❀ A householder can have it on a hanging or painting directly opposite the front door to ensure that anyone who enters with ill intent (for example, a burglar) is repelled.

❀ You can purchase small evil eye charms for pets to wear on their collars.

❀ Jewelery or keyrings are an easy way to keep the charm about your person.

Today even some high-end jewelery designers use the evil eye in their designs. It is a particularly good charm to add to a charm bracelet and is now ubiquitous and secular enough a design to wear as a necklace without comment from others.

CHILDREN AND COWS

Medieval parish records in England and Scotland give many instances of children or cattle having been especially affected by the evil eye. A child that has been affected in this way will cry for no reason or be unusually quiet and unresponsive, sometimes with half-closed eyes. Cows will also behave unusually and may cease to give milk.

In the Indian sub-continent, the evil eye can be removed with a simple ritual involving cloves.

Take five, seven or eleven closes and encircle the child (or cow!)'s head with them in an anti-clockwise direction three times and burn the cloves. This removes the evil eye and the child is back to normal shortly afterwards. If there is no smell from the burning cloves then this is seen as a proof that it was the evil eye that inflicted him or her.

Cloves are used in this way because it is believed that everything has a spirit and the spirit of cloves is the spirit of unseen matter. When cloves are used in this way, we can connect with the spirit world and warn off any evil.

The number of cloves burnt is also significant in that odd numbers are considered good while even ones are generally not. This is because when you divide even numbers into two, nothing is left, whereas there is always something remaining with odd numbers, making them good for spellwork and prosperity.

The evil eye plays a huge role in everyday rituals in the Indian sub-continent. It is common to find babies and children wearing a black thread around their necks or wrists or black eyeliner (*kajal*). Although outwardly this is to protect from the evil eye, most occultists will tell you that black is the color of Saturn, a malefic star, and wearing a black thread protects from the influence of that planet.

Our use of make-up may also have originated from a desire to avert the evil eye with evidence from ancient Egypt that women would paint their eyes and lips as protective measures. Something to think about the next time you're putting on your 'war paint'.

OTHER WAYS TO AVOID THE EVIL EYE

❃ Horseshoes over the door of a house—do ensure it is placed open side up.

❃ Scattering lentils in your front garden helps the birds and also detracts the evil eye – urad dhal (available at most Indian stores) scattered on a Saturday is particularly effective.

❃ Wearing an iron ring, ideally on your middle finger—this metal has a way of deflecting malevolence from all manner of entities and quarters.

YOUR PERSONAL CHARM

You can also create a charm that is yours personally, not bought or even created with universal symbols – a unique object made mindfully for your own protection and fortune.

Find a stone in a location that means something to you; it could be your garden or a local park or even an exotic beach on your holidays (although do check the local laws as some countries and areas prohibit you taking any stone or shell away with you). Hold the stone (or shell) in the palm of your non-dominant hand (left, if you're right-handed and right, if you're left-handed), close your eyes and see what images come into your mind.

Mentally ask the stone if it will come away with you, to help you in your life. If the answer comes back as a positive, thank the stone and take it with you. If you feel like you're getting a 'no' and the stone would prefer to stay where it is, thank it again and put it back where you found it. Once you have stone that resonates with you, you're ready to make your personal charm.

Such stone charms are inspired by thunderstones, a Haitian tradition that originates in the belief that there are powerful stones out in the world that were formed during the creation of the universe. The creation story is that when Damballah and Ayida-Wedo, the snake-gods, gave birth to all life, sparks of magic fell from them as lightning to the earth. This energy embedded itself in the landscape, producing natural places of power. Their power entered the stones of those places. That power can be accessed through painting your specific stone with intent.

When you paint your stone, you are asking the universe to manifest that desire for you. It is deeply and profoundly personal. You then reinforce your intent each time you handle your stone. You can carry a stone made for wealth in your purse, near your wallet. A stone for getting rid of nightmares can be placed under your pillow or mattress. You can make very large charm stones for your home and garden to protect your property from theft, fire or flood. Charm stones work by helping you tap into a source of universal manifestation.

Other areas you can use your personal charm stone for:

- staying safe online
- greater wealth
- finding love
- mending a broken heart
- rekindling a lapsed friendship
- finding greater health and vitality
- protecting your home
- communicating with elemental spirits and inviting them into your garden

DIFFERENT TYPES OF STONES

A couple of my friends who share my compulsion for picking up rocks, stones, pebbles and shells have told me that they forget where they got them after a while. I never do. To me, each stone and shell is a living being. I remember where they come from just as I would remember, if we were to meet, whether you were from Derbyshire or Dallas.

I also remember because I ask stones whether they are willing to come away with me. If you mentally ask the stone if it will come away with you, as suggested, you will find you get a strong 'yes' or 'no' response from this supposedly silent object.

Rocky stones

Volcanic, jagged rocks are not usually suitable for painting but are fantastic for raising the energy in your home. If you find a particularly beautiful one, you can use it without painting it for focusing 'doing' energy into you. Just remember to ask the stone if it wants to come with you and, again, if it wants to be painted if you're in any doubt.

Woodland stones

These are cool, earthy stones that take on the energy of the tree canopy above them. They are very good for calming rowdy children and for helping with stress.

River stones

These stones are fantastic for healing emotional and physical wounds and calming fevers. Whatever size your river stone is, it can bring a sense of light joy into your home. Every once in a while, take your stone to running water and wash it, it will renew its energy. You may even decide to paint your stone as a home protection one and pop it in your pond.

Sea stones

These are wild, wandering stones and you may find that these stones journey away from you, after staying a while and working their magic. They make fantastic gifts as Spirit stones because the more they change hands, the happier they will be. Don't worry about having an unhappy sea stone – they can find their own way back to the sea when they're done on land.

Mysterious stones

In the garden, in an urban pub or in your shoe, some stones turn up when you're not looking for them. Like rocky stones, these mysterious stones don't always need painting to be potent. You will know when you touch them what they're with you for. Put them on your altar or hold them when you sit in meditation – you're truly blessed if you get one.

LOVE STONES

Throughout the world there are a number of potent symbols for love. The most obvious one that we see all over the world, especially on the St. Valentine's Day, is the heart. Historically the heart has been seen as the moral center of a human being. In Egyptian mythology the heart is weighed against the feather of Maat (symbolizing truth) after a person dies. If it is heavier than the feather, it is considered to be full of sins and the person goes to hell. If it is lighter, the person is allowed to go to heaven. This may well be the origin of why we say we have a light heart when we are carefree and a heavy one when we are worried or regretful.

When exactly the heart came to be exclusively the domain of love, as opposed to morality or the intellect as it had been in the past, is unclear but modern conceptions of romantic love would be incomplete without this symbol. We say we have a broken heart when we are crossed in love and we say we give our hearts when we fall in love.

One symbol incorporating the heart is that of the Claddagh. This is a heart, held in two hands with a crown over it. It symbolizes love, friendship and loyalty. If you wear a Claddagh ring with the heart facing inwards toward you on your right hand, you indicate you are in love. If you wear it outwards, you have not yet given your heart away. If you wear it on your left hand, inwards, your love is requited. Remember this if you decorate your spirit stone with a Claddagh and, when you meditate with your stone after you have made it, hold it facing inwards in your left hand if you wish someone you love to notice you.

People come from all over the world to South West Ireland to kiss the Blarney Stone, said to bestow charm and eloquence on the kisser. Then there are the famous 'kissing' Wain stones of the Peak District. There's much kissing that goes on with and between stones so why not ask them to help you find love? Think of the stoicism of a stone when you're getting over a broken heart. Think of the steadfastness of a stone when you're despairing of ever finding 'the one'.

PROSPERITY STONES

From coins and wheat to shamrocks, there are many symbols that are said to bring luck and prosperity into your life. Kings have been crowned on stones and dragons of legend hid their treasure beneath stones. Stones with a hole worn through them by running water are considered to be exceptionally lucky fairy stones. In this section you can read legends and myths about stones and prosperity. Gain inspiration for making your own prosperity stones. Includes case studies on making money and getting rid of debt.

Home Protection Stones

Hearth stones can be the heart of your home and are said to protect it from theft, fire and flood. People have believed certain stones were imbued with the ability to repel evil. Here you can read the legends and see the symbols that will protect your own home and garden, making it a safe haven for you. Case studies on protecting the home.

Health Stones

Many stones are said to heal people physically from hot stone therapies to *Zare Mora*, a stone from the tribal regions of Baluchistan. Read the mythology around these stones and discover how to make your own stones for everything from supporting weight loss to getting more energy. Case studies on weight loss and fertility. How to create one as a gift for someone who is ill.

PAINTING YOUR CHARM

Materials
- Paintbrushes
- Acrylic paints
- Palette
- Quick drying varnish
- Old newspapers

PREPARING YOUR STONE

Wash your stone in clean water and dry it completely. Leave it overnight in a bowl of salt, covering it entirely. In the morning, brush off the salt and take your stone to your painting space.

Sit in meditation with your stone for a while and ensure that you are meant to paint it. Some stones are very beautiful in their own right and nature has done the artistry for you. The wonderful thing about stones are their generosity, you can always find another stone to paint if the one that is before you is not quite right for it.

✂ Step One

Paint your base coat. This should be the color that best corresponds to your desired outcome (see the table opposite). Ensure this coat dries completely before moving onto the next step. Try to keep your strokes in one direction and concentrate on your outcome as much as possible.

✂ Step Two

Add your pattern and symbols. This may be a two or even three stage process with you building up paint and patterns, depending on the style you want to use. Aboriginal-inspired painting, for example, uses dots to build up intricate patterns. Paint any colors on first before you do white dots to finish, ensuring you wait for each color to dry.

✂ Step Three

Once all your coats of paint are dry and you are happy with your pattern, paint varnish over your stone. This will dry to hard-wearing, glossy surface that will allow you to carry your stone around with you without damaging it.

Tips

▷ Do one side of the stone at a time so you don't smudge the other side by putting it down before it's dried.
▷ Don't restrict yourself to using brushes, you can use twigs or the end of your paintbrush to get more control in your painting.

Base colors to use

▷ Love: red, pink, purple
▷ Prosperity: green, violet
▷ Home protection: blue, black, white
▷ Health: orange, white

ETHICAL ENGAGEMENT

3

SPELLCRAFTING WELL

There is the likelihood that, as you make progress in your spellcrafting journey, others will ask you to do spells for them. There is nothing wrong with that in and of itself, but you should be aware of a few things before deciding to do spells for others. The greatest of the things you must learn is ethical engagement. This means that you never use magic to bend the will of others. That way bad things lie.

As a good and responsible practitioner of magic, you will learn how to craft spells that align to the energies of the Universe in ways that manifest great outcomes. If, at any time, you feel as though your spellwork is leading you down a path that you don't understand or enjoy, halt your practice, and journal in your Book of Shadows for a while, asking for guidance. This will ensure that you come back to your rituals with clear intent. We saw in the two earlier parts how we should keep our bodies and environments clear, clean, and conducive to the practice of magic. In this section, we have spells for you to begin to try out and within those, you will find how to attract without force and how to repel without hurting anyone.

While I don't subscribe to a three-fold return ethics, in the way that Wiccans do, I do still believe that we reap what we sow, which is why your intent has to be pure. Don't be afraid of magic. It isn't like in the movies, in that you won't suddenly raise a demon or set evil in motion. If your intent is to bring about good things for yourself and others, you will find those outcomes. The Universe is a friendly place and wants us to be happy. As long as we follow ethical rules of engagement, we are free to create whatever kind of life we want for ourselves. You can attract love, money, health, happiness, and a sense of community without taking anything away from others or needing to harm any creatures in your spellwork.

THE SPELLS

BOOK OF SHADOWS

If you're beginning your journey into magic, keep a journal of your thoughts, feelings, spells and rituals you do and outcomes – expected and unexpected – that might arise. In the movies, this is always a leather-bound tome that ends up having a significant part to play in the plot, but you can have whatever book you choose. Just pick one that you feel comfortable storing all your spellwork in.

What you'll need:

▷ A book to write in dedicated to magic work and thoughts alone
▷ A white candle

Moon Phase: New or Waxing Moon

1. Bathe and dress in a way that feels appropriate to you.

2. Light a white candle – a tealight is fine – and sit still in contemplation of the flame for a while.

3. Hold the book in your lap for a while and mentally ask Divinity or the Universe that this book helps you on your spiritual journey.

4. Open to the first page and write down the first word or sentence that comes to mind. Don't think too hard about this. Literally the first sentence. It may be a weird word or what, at first, seems a negative sentence or word. Don't censor or edit yourself.

5. Over the coming weeks keep an eye open for anything that might help you make sense of the message of your first word or sentence. Write anything that comes up down in your book.

Anyone who identifies as a witch will find that at some point he or she is met with the fear and discomfort of others. Generally speaking, this arises from an embedded idea that witches curse. Much like the wicked stepmother in fairytales, witches have also had a very bad press with respect to history and popular culture. In the west we might be able to laugh this off, but the truth is in some parts of the world even today people are being tortured and killed because they are suspected of being witches.

This fear emanates from control. People who refuse to take personal responsibility for their energetic hygiene and mental processes find it very easy to blame bad luck on external forces such as the big, bad witch. Sometimes you attract bad luck through negative thought. Sometimes an act of the gods just happens and nobody could control that happening. However, weak people take comfort from the idea that they can't help themselves because someone has cursed them. Then others take money from these folk to "remove" these curses.

Everything is alive and responsive. A spiritual teacher taught me this important fact for every witch to know. This means that the energy that flows through literally everything can be molded to certain outcomes, the very essence of spellcraft. One way in which we see this made manifest is in charms. Throughout the world there are examples of symbols worn on the person or hung in one's house for protection and to attract good luck.

The most effective charm is one you create yourself rather than buy from a job lot made, at great expense to the planet, in the cheapest place of manufacture. The simplest charm of all to make is a spell stone. A spell stone is made by first deciding exactly what it is you wish for. This could be for greater wealth, to find love, to mend a broken heart, to feel healthier, manifest a holiday or a new home… virtually anything you like as long as it is ethical.

Once you have set your intent, think of an image that conjures up the manifestation of that desire for you. For example, if you want to make a stone for love, a heart may make you think of love and you could use that as the basis for the design you'll paint onto your stone. If you find it hard to think of something, there are plenty of symbols from world beliefs to give you inspiration.

You do not have to be an artist to do this. All you have to do is concentrate on your goal while painting your stone. You may find you go into a light trance state as you're painting – this will help your intention become reality.

THUNDERSTONES

I hold the idea of thunderstones in my mind when I create a spell stone. There are thunderstone stories throughout the world to explain the shaped flintheads that people have found in the land. For example, a Haitian belief is that they are powerful stones that were formed during the creation of the universe. The creation story is that when Damballah and Ayida-Wedo, the snake-gods, gave birth to all life, sparks of magic fell from them as lightening to the Earth. This energy embedded itself in the landscape, producing natural places of power. Their power entered the stones of those places. This idea of powerful stones is found in almost all native cultures of the world.

Spell stones work on exactly the same principle. The unique thing about spell stones is that your craftwork is part of the spell. When you paint your stone, you are asking the universe to manifest that desire for you. It is deeply and profoundly personal. You then reinforce your intent each time you handle your stone. You can carry a stone made for wealth in your purse, near your wallet. A stone for getting rid of nightmares can be placed under your pillow or mattress. You can make very large spell stones for your home and garden to protect your property from theft, fire or flood. Spell stones work by helping you tap into a source of universal manifestation.

Moon Phase: This will depend on what you are making the stone for. To get rid of something, choose it on a waning moon. To attract something, choose it on a waxing or new moon.

1. Find a stone in a location that means something to you; it could be your garden or a local park or even an exotic beach on your holidays (though be aware that on some beaches, it is forbidden to remove stones). Hold the stone in the palm of your non-dominant hand (left, if you're right-handed and right, if you're left-handed), close your eyes and see what images come into your mind. Mentally ask the stone if it will come away with you, to help you in your life. If the answer comes back as a positive, thank the stone and take it with you. If you feel like you're getting a 'no' and the stone would prefer to stay where it is, also thank it and put it back where you found it. Once you have a stone that resonates with you, you're ready to make a spell stone.

2. Find a symbol that is most fitting for what you want to manifest.

3. Paint the symbol onto the stone. It could be as simple as a dot or as elaborate as you like, but making your mark seals your intent onto the stone. Carry the stone with you (if it is for personal use and not the home) and touch it regularly to remind yourself of your intent.

Have you heard about the cleaning and tidying craze sweeping the world at the minute? From Mrs Hinch to Marie Kondo, everybody seems to be going loopy for putting away things and cleaning surfaces. I suppose it stems from feeling like you can't control some of the awful things happening in the world and so you can at least control your own space.

I am a huge advocate for clearing your head by clearing your space, however, I do think that we sometimes don't join the dots up in our heads when we think about cleanliness. Let me give you an example. Who is dirtier – the fragrant person who has applied creams, deodorant and perfume to their body or the showered with simple handmade soap one who nevertheless still has the faintest tang of natural body odor? In the first instance, on a monthly basis, that person is going to be discarding plastics and contributing through factory processes to a strain on resources and ensuring at every point of the chain that pollution is being put out into the world.

What is ickier – using a menstrual cup or putting sanitary towels and tampons into landfill each month? We have to make those decisions based not just on our personal convenience but on what we are leaving as our legacy on Earth.

INNER CONFLICT

Following a plant-based diet is one of the best things you can do for the planet. Not taking flights and not keeping a car are other ways to be kinder to the world around you. We know all these things, but convenience can drive behaviors that don't align with our true values. When that happens, we create tension in our bodies. We are at war with ourselves.

This year it has been wonderful to see young people earnestly telling the world that they want a future devoid of the mess and dirt that our unfettered consumption has created. They have inconvenienced us by blocking roads and stopping trains. This is necessary in order to align us to our true values. Nobody wants a barren, dead planet. That makes the issue at hand bigger than whether police have canceled leave or workers make it to the office in time. It is not an exaggeration to say that police, offices and roads for that matter won't exist if we don't stop climate change.

As witches, we attempt to step into our power and that can often be decisions at such a micro level that outsiders won't even recognize it as the exercise of power and will. However, it is at this atomic level that change truly happens. If we align to our values and behave in a way that is congruent with our beliefs, the universe strives to help us get the outcomes we desire.

PRACTICAL MAGIC

When you sit and think about your values, what do you think of? Who are you? What do you care deeply about? Once you hold in your mind the very best of who you are, you can begin to take steps to ensure that you are being true to yourself. Don't worry about changing those around you – and don't verbally caption everything you're doing. Just begin to reject anything that doesn't hold true to your values and accept that which aligns to them.

Be kind to yourself and others. The process of aligning to your values is a journey and not a destination so you won't get there immediately. Beating yourself up for needing to take a flight or having to buy a bottle of water is not helpful or even fair. If you are thinking deeply about these matters, that is already more than many of our politicians and leaders are doing so stay on course. This way magic lies!

MAGICAL NATURAL DEODORANT RECIPE

Moon Phase: Any

This potion is both practical and magical. If the bicarb causes you skin problems, you can leave it out entirely. Use only a thin layer as a little goes a long way.

- ▷ 6 tbsp coconut oil
- ▷ 4 tbsp bicarbonate of soda
- ▷ 4 tbsp cornflour
- ▷ Your favorite essential oil

1. Mix the bicarbonate of soda and cornflour together in a bowl. Then mash in the coconut oil until completely mixed together. Add a drop or two of your favorite essential oil.

2. Hold the idea of how you want to walk in the world in your mind, whether that is seductive or gentle or glowing with daily magic. Blow your intention three times into the bowl. Store in a clean, airtight container; a small kilner jar is excellent for this as it allows you to have easy access to the deodorant.

Witches are more visible during celebrations and high holidays. The mainstream press loves gleefully showing an attractive sky-clad female witch doing a Litha ritual at summer solstice. And there's always the annual article in the national newspapers about how a 'real' witch celebrates Samhain. But what about everyday life? Witches are also people with all the same needs and worries as everyone else.

The truth is that life doesn't always lend itself to magic and enchantment. Making the beds, doing the dishes, sorting the laundry, remembering to pay bills and take out the rubbish… all the hundreds of chores we have in a given week; this is the daily round that makes up our lives and can crush all the wonder out of us if we let it.

I was once told by a spiritual teacher that you can create and destroy universes in the kneading of bread. I understood the truth of that the next time I was making bread. The reason mindfulness is now so popular is that people can see the impact that giving your attention to daily tasks has. Part of my witchcraft practice is ensuring that I bring that level of attention and awareness to everything I do. When I take out the recycling I do it with gratitude for the fact that I have been able to afford those items and that the technology exists for any waste put into the recycling to be used again. I make the bed to honor the spirit of the space in my bedroom and all the entities that live there. I can sense how much more of a happy place it is once it is tidy and clean.

LOSING YOUR SPARKLE

It is easy when you have demands on your time and energy to forget about ritual and spell-work. Suddenly you have no idea what phase the moon is in and it has been weeks since you did anything magical. You might even start feeling depressed and wondering what it's all for anyway. This is the time to stop and rebalance yourself. The dense energy of the world is clinging to you and weighing you down. When this happens to me, one of the first things I do is a radical declutter. I begin by limiting to almost zero my interaction with news or social media. This is temporary but a day or two off it reminds me to trust my own intuition and not get blown about by various opinions and standpoints.

I then go through a physical declutter and cleanse my space. Then I visualize a golden sparkling energy coming in through my front door (even if closed) and whooshing through the flat, clearing away anything that isn't meant to be there. Finally, I stick on a movie that I find magically inspiring. While films such as Practical Magic or The Mummy don't contain any real occult knowledge, the scenery, the costumes and the sheer fun of the endeavor serve to bring me back to remembering magic.

Doing these little things sparks something that returns me to myself. It may not work for everyone and sometimes you don't even have the energy to do anything (be kind to yourself when that happens), but it is a plan to begin the process of re-enchantment.

Another vital cure for the mundane blues is to get out in nature. Dragonflies become fairies in disguise. Trees speak to you in rustling voices. That rabbit that darts out across your path has a message for you, as does the fox following swiftly behind it. Brother Crow wants you to be happy. And spending time with all these elements might just get you there.

RE-ENCHANTING THE WORLD PRAYER

Moon phase: Waxing

▷ Candle: white or gold

1. Sit where you won't be disturbed for a while, ideally in front of your altar.

2. Light the candle.

3. Close your eyes and place your hands, palms facing upwards, beside you or in your lap.

4. Call on the god or goddess you most affiliate with to guide you. Ask what you should do to make your experience of life more magical.

5. Sit in this space for a while, thinking about the answers that you are being given.

6. Then turn your palms downwards and rub them against your legs and open your eyes.

7. Write down the answers you've been given.

8. Review your answers two weeks later and see how they relate to what has happened over the last fortnight.

Now that you have opened the doors of communication with your divine guide, you will also find that you receive powerful, transforming dreams and strange, delightful coincidences.

The word occult means hidden. I recall when I used to edit a magazine that covered the occult; there was much nervousness with the publisher who thought occult meant virgin sacrifices and drinking of blood etc. ("only on weekends and high holidays", I quipped in response). I have been thinking about the literal meaning of occult quite a bit recently. I follow a number of witchcraft hashtags on social media and I regularly see people posting up photos of their altars, workings, and spellwork in detail. I understand that this is a way of connecting with others interested in witchcraft, but I do think the solitary practitioners I trained with would be horrified at the openness with which esoteric matters are now discussed. Part of me sees the benefit to it as you can feel very isolated if your family, birth religion, or society rejects your personal beliefs and this can be a way to get validation and not feel so alone.

The flip side, however, is that you lay everything open and in some traditions that results in energy and power ebbing away just as the sacredness of the moment does. If you stop in the midst of your working to take a photo for social media, is it still as powerful a working done privately and with only the participants present? I don't know the answer to that, but I have made a decision recently to step back from social media in order to reinstate the boundary between the public and the private.

LOVE YOURSELF SPELL

Moon phase: Waxing or full

▷ Candle: pink or red

1. Sit where you won't be disturbed for a while, ideally in front of your altar.

2. Light the candle.

3. Close your eyes and place your hands, palms facing upwards, beside you or in your lap.

4. Call on the god or goddess you most affiliate with to guide you. Ask what you should do to treat yourself with more love and respect. You cań use a clean page in your Book of Shadows to record any spontaneous answers that arise for you.

5. Sit in this space for a while, thinking about the answers that you are being given.

6. Then turn your palms downwards and rub them against your legs and open your eyes.

7. Write down the answers you've been given.

8. Review your answers two weeks later and see how they relate to what has manifested.

You can adapt this spell to also work in a spell to attract a partner. In such a case, you ask your deities (or the Universe, if you prefer a more secular approach) to bring you the love you seek in the form of another, rather than asking what you can do to love yourself more.

One of the most important things to remember when doing love spells of any kind is that you should not attempt to bend the will of others. It is fine to think about the qualities you admire in a particular person when constructing your spell, but asking the Universe or your chosen deities to deliver a specific person to you is both unethical and unlikely to happen.

I have known some very powerful witches who in their youth and inexperience did spells to attract a specific person and found that there were unforeseen consequences—for example, that the person was not who they thought they were or that they weren't able to commit in the way they had hoped. Such relationships end messily and unhappily, so it is always best to ensure that you do spells that are for the highest good of all rather than to bend the will of others to you.

You can also use visual or olfactory aspects to make a spell more charged. An altar scattered with red roses or burning rose essential oil will put you in the right frame of mind for a love spell. Consider placing anything on your altar that represents love for you, whether that is a small sculpture of two birds together or two ribbons tied together. I used a circlet of ivy when manifesting my husband and, two years later, our hands were bound together with ivy by the Pagan priest in our handfasting ceremony.

COSMIC CONNECTION SPELL

Moon phase: Waxing

▷ Candle: white, silver, or gold

1. Sit where you won't be disturbed for a while, ideally in front of your altar.

2. Light the candle.

3. Close your eyes and place your hands, palms facing upwards, beside you or in your lap.

4. Call on the god or goddess you most affiliate with to guide you. Then imagine a light coming from above to the top of your head. Allow yourself to be guided as to the color of the light. This will also have significance for your spell. For example, the color green might suggest that you go out into nature more to re-establish your connection with the cosmos. Alternatively, it might be blue to suggest going to visit the deities of the sea or up a mountain or hill for spirits of the air.

5. Sit in this space for a while, thinking about the images and ideas that you are being given.

6. Then turn your palms downwards and rub them against your legs and open your eyes.

7. Write down your thoughts in your Book of Shadows, adding any aspects you added to the spell by way of energy manipulation or extra ingredients or items on your altar. Remember, as we have said before, that you must make your spell unique to you. You might chant or say a charm, you might consecrate an object

to carry with you, or you might just sit in meditation for a while.

8. Review your work two weeks later and see how things have turned out over the last fortnight. Do you feel more connected or are you still feeling blocked? If the latter, consider repeating the spell in a month's time, asking for more specific guidance on where your disconnection lies.

To be connected to the cosmos is already the status of every living being. You are connected, even if you feel disconnected. This spell is more about allowing you to experience the pure joy of knowing that you are a spiritual being and are part of the Great Mystery.

This and the *Re-enchanting The World Prayer* (page 90) may seem to be very esoteric and not necessarily the sort of spells you might think about when you first begin practicing witchcraft, but they are among the most important. To have power to make effective spells, you need to be aligned with both the spiritual and material worlds. Trying to cause material effects without first addressing the spiritual will only make your spells a damp squib. Vice versa, too much emphasis on the spiritual is dishonest, because we are material beings living in a material world. To pretend that an intense connection to the Divine is in any way useful if you haven't the money to pay your bills or buy food is simply incorrect. Saints and monks might disagree, but most of us can't be sustained by spiritual experiences alone. So ensure your practice has a strong spiritual foundation but builds on material outcomes.

KEY TO WEALTH SPELL

Moon phase: Waxing (or waning if you're getting rid of debts)

▷ Candle: green or gold
▷ Ingredients: Basil leaf, basil oil, gold pen, an old key or key charm, fireproof bowl

1. Sit where you won't be disturbed for a while, ideally in front of your altar.

2. Light the candle. Write the number and currency of how much you want to manifest in the gold ink on the basil leaf. You should do a calculation before the spell to arrive at a figure that would comfortably resolve your financial problems.

3. Close your eyes and place your hands in your lap, with the old key or key charm closed in your right palm.

4. Call on the god or goddess you most affiliate with, or the Universe, to help power your spell. Say your own words to this effect: "As basil burns, it takes my plea up to the heavens, I ask that wealth comes to me, as holder of the key."

5. Then burn the basil leaf in the fireproof bowl, passing the key through the smoke.

6. Once the basil leaf has burned away, kiss the key and place it in your wallet or in the pocket of a coat or jacket you wear daily.

7. Write down the date and details of what you did and the request you made in your Book of Shadows.

8. Review your answers two weeks later and see whether you can see any green shoots with regard to your finances.

After love, money is the spellwork I am most asked to do. Finances can be tricky at the best of times, but the most important aspect of wealth spells is responsibility.

You have to take responsibility for your situation. This isn't the same as blame. If you are responsible for everything that happens to you, you have the power to change it. If you are merely the victim of your circumstances, buffeted around by the winds of fate, you won't have the energetic power to change your world. You have to accept responsibility before you can effect lasting change.

For example, if you have significant debts, you must acknowledge that you decided to spend the money that caused the debt. Now you might have had very good reasons for doing so—for example, having to pay rent or for a medical procedure—so you're not to blame for the debt, but you are responsible for it. This doesn't mean you sit and berate yourself for your spending on designer shoes or champagne. You just accept that this is something you brought into being and state your intent to release that outcome and bring a new one into your life.

SPELL TO MEND A BROKEN HEART

Moon phase: Waning

▷ Candle: Black or white
▷ Ingredients: a bowl of fresh water

1. Sit where you won't be disturbed for a while, ideally in front of your altar.

2. Light the candle and sit with the bowl of water in front of you.

3. Close your eyes and think about the heartache you are experiencing. Think about what it is that you fear from the loss of a relationship or the conflict or challenge you are facing. Then, as that feeling builds in your chest, blow it out into the bowl of water. Visualize it as smoke leaving your lungs and going into the water.

4. Take the bowl to your toilet and pour the water away, imagining that your heartache is being flushed away with the water.

5. Sit in meditation for a while, rubbing your belly to comfort yourself.

6. In future, if you start to feel overwhelmed with sadness, gently rub your stomach and

remind yourself that you are stronger than any challenge you face.

7. Write down the date of your spell in your Book of Shadows.

8. A year from now, look back on your entry for that date and see how much your feelings about things have changed. You will find that you are no longer plagued by the heartbreak.

There are many rituals and spells that deal with getting rid of a broken heart, but please don't forget that emotional pain is part of the human condition. Sometimes you are guided in spellwork and meditation to sit with your pain. This can be a horrible prospect, but sometimes the healing comes from acknowledging that you are unhappy and that it is fine to be so for a while. It is only when it tips into a way of life that you must intervene with yourself and take steps to regain your sense of self without sorrow.

FIND YOUR SOUL GROUP SPELL

Moon phase: Waxing

▷ Candle: blue or gold
▷ Tools: red thread

1. Sit where you won't be disturbed for a while, ideally in front of your altar.

2. Light the candle.

3. Close your eyes and place your hands, palms facing upwards, beside you or in your lap.

4. Call on the Universe or the god or goddess you most affiliate with to guide you. Think about the sort of spiritual community you would like to be a part of, whether that is part of a formal organization such as a church or temple, or whether that is an informal group of friends pursuing the same goals.

5. Having formed in your mind the sort of group you would like to be a part of, open your eyes and turn your palms downwards and rub them against your legs. Then take the thread and tie a knot in it for every member of the group you are envisioning. Say something along the

lines of: "Come to me in love and harmony, come to me for purposes pure, come to me, my soul group all, that we may begin our healing work." Then take the thread and tie one end to the other so that it is a circle or loop. Put it safely in a drawer or closet where it won't be disturbed.

6. Notice who comes into your life over the coming weeks. Examine your feelings about them. Your soul group will feel like you've known them forever and there will be an instant connection because you are already connected spiritually.

7. If you move away from the group or community and feel that you need to gently let go of the binds between you, cut each knot out and then bury the thread in your garden or in a place where it will biodegrade without littering.

Some witches work in covens because they know about the power of soul groups. While I have always been a solitary witch, I do have a soul group of other solitary witches and we exchange ideas, spells, recipes, and magical information on a regular basis. Humans need connection and so, if you feel disconnected from your soul group and feel like you need more people in your magical life, this is a good way of attracting them back to you.

Be aware that group dynamics can sometimes be a bit challenging, in that some times you will disagree on how to proceed with an idea or act. This is absolutely fine as you are not aiming to become carbon copies of each other and you do not need to agree on everything. The important thing is that you treat everyone with love and respect so that your magical work is at its highest level.

FAIRY HELP SPELL

Moon phase: Any

▷ Tools: pen, paper, small cake and a drink of something pleasing

1. Find a place outdoors in which you feel particularly connected to nature. Woodland would be ideal, but perhaps a waterfall or even an urban park will work.

2. Take your pen and paper and write down what you need help with. Be as clear and direct as possible. So if you want to buy a house, state the amount you want your mortgage approved for, the area you want to live in, the number of bedrooms etc.

3. Close your eyes and place your hands, palms facing upwards, beside you or in your lap.

4. Call on the fairies to help you. State either out loud or in your mind that you respect their power and would love to have their help.

5. Sit for a while, thinking about how delightful it will be when your wish has come true. Really feel the emotions of having whatever your heart desires manifest for you.

6. Then turn your palms downwards and rub them against your legs and open your eyes.

7. Go to a tree or a fern bush and plant the folded paper into the soil. Leave the cake at the site and pour a little of the drink on the soil.

8. When the help has been given, don't forget to come back and give thanks at the place where you asked for help. You can return with more cake and drink, or perhaps leave a small charm or sparkly object for the fairies to enjoy.

Fairies are considered by some to be the old gods, that humans stopped worshiping in modern times. Others think they may be nature spirits. Just like people, not all are helpful, but those who are will give many blessings to their favored friends. So you should always treat any fairy with respect and good manners.

Some tales tell of frightening encounters and we have the old advice of never stepping into a fairy ring and never eating or drinking anything in the fairy realm. This is always good advice, but it doesn't work the other way round as the fairies love our food and drink, and they are helpful creatures when they have a mind to be so.

As an aside, a good protection against malevolent fairies is iron, in the shape of a used horseshoe or an iron ring. It is for this reason that you should avoid communing with fairies wearing or carrying anything made of iron.

ENCHANT BY CANDLELIGHT SPELL

Moon phase: Any

▷ Candle: Any

1. Begin a daily ritual of lighting one or three candles in the color of your choice.

2. Sit looking at the candle and soften your gaze.

3. Think about which enchantments you wish to bring forth that day. It may be how you want to be perceived by others (for example, as a good candidate in a job interview or a funny person if you're doing an open mic stand-up that evening) or it may be which experiences you want to attract that day.

4. As you gaze at the candlelight, say "Bring forth this by candlelight, bring forth this by my birthright," and cup your hand a bit above the candle and scoop the energy from its flame up to your third eye. Be careful not to get too close to the candle to burn, you are just taking the energy of its light way above the flame. Do this three times.

5. Sit in meditation for a while, thinking about what your day holds and what the best

outcome for each of your interactions with others would be. Be confident that this is precisely how things will play out today.

6. Thank the Universe or whichever god or goddess you worship for always protecting and helping you. Then blow out the candle(s).

7. Ensure the candles you use for this enchantment purpose are always kept separately from everyday candles used simply to give light or ambiance to a room. These are your magical tools and should be kept apart from household items.

To enchant means to put under a spell, but it also means to charm or delight in an ordinary sense. As such, enchanting can be delighting the world around you as much as it is imposing your will upon it. This is important to keep in mind as you go about your day. Are you behaving in a way that will charm and delight those around you or are you behaving discordantly?

When you build up a daily practice of attempting to enchant the world around you, you will find that things become easier. Opportunities come your way that you were not expecting. People are helpful in ways that surprise you. Life might not turn into a Disney film with bluebirds chirping away and everything being sweetness and light, but you will find that the world is more inclined toward blessing you with small acts of kindness and luck. Return that blessing with gratitude. Oscar Wilde said, "Some people cause happiness wherever they go; others, whenever they go." Try to be the former kind of person. Add to universal happiness instead of taking away from it.

HEARTH AND HOME SPELL

Moon phase: Any

▷ Candle: Blue
▷ Tools: besom or broom

1. Light a candle and sit in meditation in front of it for a while, thinking about your home.

2. Make a mental list of what you think would make your home a more comfortable and welcoming space.

3. Call on Hestia, the goddess of hearth and home, to bless your dwelling and keep everyone in it safe and sound.

4. Commit to blessing your home with cleanliness and ceremoniously sweep each room in your home, working out toward the front door. Once you have gathered all the dust, dirt or simply dead energy at the threshold of your front door, either sweep it outside or vacuum it up at the threshold and empty your vacuum bag immediately and get it out of your house.

5. Sit in your swept space for a while and see how it feels. Note down any insights that come to you in your Book of Shadows.

The home is the most important place for a spellcrafter. This is where you will do your magic, manifest your joys, and find a haven from the world outside. Irrespective of how large your home is, or whether you own it or rent it, it is a space that should be harmonious for you and, if it is not, you have to instigate the changes it requires.

It is often said that cleanliness is next to godliness. This simply means that the energy of a space changes when it is clean and it enables a better connection to the spiritual world. So your first act after doing this ritual should be to deep clean your home.

After you have cleaned your home thoroughly, walk through each room with your palms out in front of you and "feel" what is happening energetically in each room. Does an area feel "sticky" or unhappy in some way? Look at what is there. Do you need to declutter something? Or move a heavy piece of furniture out? Does a possession kept there inspire sadness in you due to memories or even for no reason at all? Look to your intuition to figure out exactly what is going on and where the unhappiness might lie. Remedy the situation in the best way you can and then sprinkle some salt in the area. Leave it for 24 hours and then vacuum it up, emptying your vacuum bag immediately and throwing it out of the house.

You do not need to become a minimalist to have an energetically happy home. Some maximalists have wonderfully comfortable and inviting homes because they surround themselves with things they love and they honor them by keeping them clean and maintained. If this is you, you do not need to declutter, just be honest about whether you can manage to keep all your things clean, well-loved, and well-used.

COPING WITH ANXIETY MEDITATION

Moon phase: Any

▷ Candle: white

1. Sit where you won't be disturbed for a while.

2. Light the candle.

3. Close your eyes and place your hands, palms facing upwards, beside you or in your lap.

4. Call on the Universe or the god or goddess you most affiliate with to guide you. Breathe in and out gently and with control.

5. Sit in this space for a while, thinking about any images that arise. You may find that you are constantly being shown something, an animal or a place. After the meditation you can look this up. For example, I used to see a snow leopard in this meditation and discovered that snow leopards are most active in the twilight or just before dawn. I found that if I also started working at that time, my anxiety was much less intense and I felt more able to cope. You will receive some good clues to your own energy make-up in this meditation. Be sure to stay alert to them.

6. When you are done meditating, turn your palms downwards and rub them against your legs and open your eyes.

7. Write down the answers you've been given in your Book of Shadows.

Anxiety is something that can affect any one of us. You will find people in all manner of positions feeling anxious and fearful. Some of them will have jobs in which they must remain calm and they will find different ways to cope. The most successful of them know that the best way to cope with anxious thoughts is to shift your mindset. Using mind-altering substances such as alcohol to try and cope with stress and anxiety is not a proper fix. Sure, you may feel relaxed briefly, but the anxiety comes back worse than before. The best way to move out of the fight-or-flight response is to remind your body that you are not in any danger. Even if you're having a tough time at work or feel like you can't cope with family life and the demands of young children, you need to remind your body that it is in no imminent danger, it is just sensibly reacting to perceived danger.

Try doing this meditation regularly to gain the information you need in order to have a more relaxed and serene experience of life.

HEALTH AND HAPPINESS POTiON

Moon phase: Any

▷ Ingredients: a large mug of water, 1 herbal tea bag of your choice, 1 tsp dried rose petals, 1 tsp honey, juice of half a lemon, a piece of ginger (unless your preferred herbal tea already has it)

1. Sit where you won't be disturbed for a while, ideally in front of your altar. Light a candle or incense to remind yourself that you are engaging in spellcraft now.

2. Boil the water in a kettle, pan or the microwave. Add in all the ingredients and stir in a clockwise direction to bring in happiness. Visualize the potion filling with light and being infused with happiness and health.

3. Strain out the ginger, rose petals and any pips from the lemon.

4. Drink the potion, while thinking about how it can heal your body, mind, and spirit. Say words to the effect of: "Potion warm, potion bright, set all things within me right."

5. After finishing the drink, take a moment to express gratitude for the potion and its healing energy.

Remember to be cautious about any allergies when choosing your herbal tea. You can infuse any drink with healing properties, simply by concentrating on the light that you put into it. This is, of course, not a replacement for medical help when you need it, but it is a good pick-me-up for when you are feeling fatigued and low in energy.

A word on alcohol here. Some witches will use wine or mead in ceremonies and rituals. This is fine, but do remember that alcohol changes energy in a ritual. It is a mind-altering substance, even in small doses. If you want to keep a clear head, you should avoid it. If you want to put yourself in a trance state, you can do so without alcohol. This is not to say that there is anything wrong with those who incorporate alcohol into their rituals, merely that beginners should ensure they know their own energy and are comfortable with their powers before they use it.

Some practitioners always allow an "angels or ancestors' share" whenever they drink any potion or substance. This requires pouring a little of what you're drinking on the ground or in a separate glass. The energy of that drink is offered to your spirit allies. It is a friendly gesture that can ensure you are always aligned to your spiritual "team" and are always thinking of them.

WISH COME TRUE SPELL

Moon phase: Waxing

▷ Candle: white
▷ Ingredients: A dandelion clock if it is in season or some paper if it is not the season for dandelion seeds

1. Sit where you won't be disturbed for a while, ideally out of doors in your garden.

2. Light the candle. You may need a lantern of some sort to avoid the wind blowing out the candle.

3. Hold the dandelion clock in your hand and think about what it is you are wishing for. Is it for the highest good? Will it make you happy? If so, hold the vision of it coming true in your mind's eye and blow the dandelion seeds off the stalk. If you do not have a dandelion clock, write out your wish on a piece of paper. Light the paper on your candle and let it burn away in a fireproof bowl, letting the ashes float away on the wind.

4. Sit in contemplation of your desires for a while and perhaps journal your thoughts about how you think your life will be when your wish has come true.

You can wish your life away. Always craving for what isn't is a surefire way toward unhappiness, but playful wishing, a sense of whimsy that children naturally have, is a positive manifestation of wishing. You should aim for that sort of energy whenever you are doing spells for wishes to come true.

The most important part of that spell is thinking and envisioning what life will be like once that wish has come true. Will you then immediately move on to wanting something else? Will you enjoy your boon with gratitude and pass on your good fortune to others? Is your wish for the good of everyone involved or a desire that only you have?

This spell requires you to be outside. Witches often find that any sort of spell done outdoors has to be more carefully planned so that others do not interfere or affect the spellcrafter. This is a problem when you do not have a large garden or private outdoor space. There are powerful spaces that witches and mages use in their magic, but you usually find that they cast an invisibility spell to avoid prying eyes coming to see what is going on. Some are proud of their magical work and have no problem with openly telling people what they are doing. I would say to start small and perhaps don't say any charms out loud if you think you'll be overheard. As you progress, you may feel more comfortable saying charms and spells out loud. Remember that prejudice still exists against witches so ensure that you feel safe with whatever you are showing to the world.

PRIVATE SPHERE

I publicly write on witchcraft and have spoken at the Pagan Federation as well as a number of Pagan festivals so I am not entirely hidden or silent about my beliefs. However, I want to create a sacred space at this time that is populated by the only person I do workings with – myself. As a solitary practitioner you do sometimes have to embrace the solitary, no matter how uncomfortable it feels. The ego wants you to let everyone know how powerful you are and you may even be excited about the wonderful results you are manifesting. However, we would do well to remember that all our folklore and mythology has taboos against revealing secrets, turning back to look or telling a real name. We even say that you shouldn't tell anyone your wish when blowing out your birthday candles because it doesn't come true if you do.

Beyond the mystical reasons for secrecy, there is still a need in life for privacy. If there wasn't, we'd all be snapchatting our bowel movements or sharing our pin numbers with strangers. I was shocked recently to receive a new bank card with the message on the card it was mounted on saying 'please don't share a photo of your new card on social media'. I try not to be judgmental but I did wonder what level of stupidity has now entered society. Clearly enough people had done that to warrant the printing of the message.

I did an experiment and avoided social media for a few days to see what, if any, changes happened. I noticed that my spellwork deepened as my focus had improved. My interactions with friends improved because I wasn't just appreciating what I already knew about their lives from social media; I was finding out what they'd been up to first hand and it was far more entertaining to be told in person than on a wee screen. It also led me to create clearer boundaries between close friends and acquaintances. The energy in maintaining connections with people who would have normally just fallen to the wayside in the days before social media is quite intense. While clicking 'like' takes but a second, your mind takes on board a connection to a person you may not 'like' very much at all.

Finally, I noticed my heart chakra felt better in meditation, as though the emotional impact of scrolling mindlessly had made my energy sluggish and muddy and it was finally clear.

Some find social media a lifeline, especially if mobility and isolation is a problem, and I'm not saying that jettisoning it is an option – or even right – for everyone, but I do know that I am now done with it.

HIDDEN SPELL

Moon phase: Waning

▷ Candle color: white

Take the petals from 8 white flowers (not roses) and put in a bowl in front of you on your altar. Light the candle and take a deep breath in and then out through your nose. Pick up the bowl and pass it counter-clockwise three times (as if making a circle vertically in the air in front of the candle). Blow three times into the bowl, imagining that all the talk and connections that no longer serve you are being blown into the bowl. Give thanks to your patron deity and sit in meditation a while. Blow out the candle and discard the petals in your garden, compost heap or anywhere else they will break down naturally.

RESULTS AND RECHARGING

WORKING TO ATTRACT

Altars are not just religious arrangements, they are increasingly used by people to create a beautiful focus for their daily meditations. The interest in subjects like Feng Shui and Vastu Shastra has also led some to experiment with using altars as manifestation tools. This means that you can create altars that bring love or money into your life. It's simply a matter of identifying where in your home a suitable altar to love or material abundance could be set up and what to put on it.

Altars gives you an idea of the depth of variety there is when creating an altar. You can use all the senses to create a really special tool for focusing the mind. Your sense of sight takes in beautiful colors and objects, you smell sweet incense and aromatic smoke, you can partake of delicious offerings that you share with the deity that you have dedicated your altar to and you can place a bell, singing bowl or wind chime before your altar that can transport you to another space and time. By placing tactile objects like stones and shells on your altar, you can also use your sense of touch to lose yourself in the patterns of the universe. In short your altar is a place of stimulation, where you connect with the greater life of the universe and all that is part of it.

Creating your altar is a meditative process and this book also shows you how to find special objects for your altar by questing for them. Then you are shown how to put an altar together and lastly how to work with it to meet your spiritual and practical goals.

OCCASIONS WHERE YOU MIGHT NEED EXTRA HELP

'Hatches, matches and dispatches' is a humorous way to describe the three main times you may need extra help in the form of protection charms. Births and babies always need extra protection to ensure a smooth birth for baby and child and then a healthy, robust childhood for the wee 'hatchling'. Weddings can be a stressful time with expectations and fears running high so we want to create some comfort and reassurance in the run-up to the big day. Then we have rituals around death to ensure the safe passage of the soul of loved ones to the afterlife but also to heal the people left behind.

Depending on your belief system, you can use angelic sigils, universal shapes or even sit in meditation and find your own symbols that arise when you think about the upcoming event. It can be lovely to make a charm for a friend or family member, but always ask permission first as the person you are making it for may not want something that doesn't fit in with their belief systems. Don't be offended if the answer is a 'no' – consent is one of the most important parts of living together in the world and we should all be wary of forcing our beliefs onto others.

❀ Births – again, if you have permission for it, it can be a great thing to sew particular charms into a baby blanket. This then becomes a wonderful heirloom that will be treasured for years once the baby is all grown up.

❀ Weddings – if the wedding party is up for it, you can consider making personal charms as part of the hen or stag do. A bit of crafting earlier in the day (for example painting stones or carving wooden amulets) can create a shared bond that makes the celebrations later in the evening go really well.

❀ Funerals – a small stone or clover from near the grave of a loved one can be painted or pressed into a book and made into a remembrance charm to bring comfort when you are grieving.

OTHER TIMES OF NEED

✼ A job search and/or interview can go better if you write exactly what you want to feel in your new job on a small bit of paper and wear it in a locket around your neck. You will energetically tell the universe what you want to manifest.

✼ If you're heading out to a party and are nervous about speaking to new people, consider wearing a blue scarf or ribbon as a charm around your neck to open up your throat chakra and make communication easier.

✼ If you're feeling a bit run-down and have already checked with your medical professional that there isn't an underlying health issue, then consider drawing out the symbol for Mars and taping it to a clear water bottle. Use filtered water in the bottle and see if this increases your energy levels. If you find that you're getting into more disputes, add the symbol for Venus next to it to balance out the energies.

There is an ancient belief that everything on heaven and earth is connected and influences each other. The Sufis call this 'Unity of Being' (*wahdat al wujud*). The meditation over the next few pages is based on this principle. It is a way of using the positive energies of stars to dissolve any limitations or negative influences in your life. So you can improve your experience of life down here on earth through a re-adjustment and revitalization of your natal horoscope on a spiritual plane.

For beginners you don't need to know the ins and outs of the planets you were born under. Simply look at the associations with each planet to find out which stars you need to focus on. Alternatively you can do this meditation for general health and happiness without needing to combat a particular problem.

All the stars have their own particular energies, both positive and negative, which are reflected in a natal chart. For example, Venus' positive energies represent love, friendship, harmony, sympathy, a social life, an artistic nature etc. However if Venus is sitting in an uncomfortable place in the birth chart or Venus is afflicted (which means if other planets are sitting opposite or at right angles to it in the sky), then it may manifest itself as over-sensitivity, laziness, superficiality, a false self-image, arrogance, indulgence, excessive sexuality, extravagance etc. Using this meditation you can learn to turn such negative traits into positive ones.

HOW To DO THE MEDiTATiON

Start the meditation on a Sunday because Sunday is ruled by the Sun, which plays the central role in Star Therapy. Also start during a waxing moon when it's on its emerging journey as this is good for starting anything new. This is a 49 day practice, split into seven day sections to enable you to take time away from the meditation if you need to. You shouldn't however stop in the midst of the seven day cycle as you will have to go back to the beginning of that cycle before you can continue with the meditation. This initial practice is based on seven stars (actually six planets and one satellite, the moon, but let's not quibble).

Make sure you are sitting comfortably and that you won't be disturbed for at least 30 minutes. Get as relaxed as possible. Ensure your spine is straight, either sitting or lying down, and take 11 deep breaths. Close your eyes, Imagine that at your solar plexus, within your body, there is a space. Once you can visualize that, think about the Sun. Imagine that from your crown all the positive energy, orange light and color of the Sun is coming down through you to your solar plexus. Increase that energy, really visualize it and gather it up. Once it forms a critical mass, it will become a small sun based at the point of your solar plexus.

This internal sun will then be giving energy to your entire body. Feel that energy coursing through you. Imagine that the light from this sun is dissolving your internal complexes, inhibitions and worries. The build up of light and energy should be so great that it begins to come out of your pores and into your aura. Anything dark in your aura is evaporated by this internal light. After this, ask the sun to stay with you forever and thank the sun for being within you. Finish the meditation and rise relaxed and full of energy. You need to do this entire process for seven consecutive days. If, in the course of your daily life, you require more energy, imagine a positive vibration from your internal sun giving you power and energy.

The next 'star' you'll need to draw down is the moon. You do the same meditation, this time altering the color you imagine to the white of the moon. When the energies of the moon are coming down from your crown, imagine that they are flowing into your internal sun. When they mingle, it is not a crash but a relaxed, happy and positive union of color and energy. When you speak to the moon at the end of the meditation, request that it stay with you forever and thank it as well. The body of light you have in you now contains sun and moon energies. If during the meditation you feel a tickling sensation or shudders, this is a sign that energies are entering you and you should not be alarmed.

You then go through each of the following stars for seven days each, mixing the colors and energies of each star within your internal ball of light. See below for the colors of the stars and their respective areas of influence. You may find it helpful to print this page out for easy reference.

THE SUN

The Sun governs sunlight and all vital forces that stem from it and flow through the solar system, allowing life to exist.

- ▷ Color: Orange
- ▷ Stones: diamonds, ruby, carbuncle
- ▷ The Sun signifies power, authority, pride, ambition, will and desire.
- ▷ Health: it rules the heart, circulation, arteries, eyes, spinal cord and the vital life force.

THE MOON

The Moon signifies mothers and women generally. Water and liquid are governed by this star too.

- ▷ Color: Silvery white
- ▷ Stones: moonstone, opals, milk-white stones
- ▷ The Moon governs feelings, sensations and instincts.
- ▷ Health: stomach and digestion, bladder, breasts, womb, child-bearing, the female cycle, the nervous system.

MERCURY

Mercury signifies schools and places of learning. It governs the intellect and education.

- ▷ Color: yellow
- ▷ Stones: topaz, agate, marble
- ▷ Mercury rules thought and reason, all intellectual faculties including articulation and communication.
- ▷ Health: the brain and nervous system, the tongue and organs of speech, hands.

VENUS

Venus signifies beauty, love, luxury, wealth and pleasure.

▷ Color: indigo
▷ Stones: Jade, lapis lazuli, beryl
▷ Venus governs the emotions and affections, particularly romantic love. Venus also governs good taste and aesthetics.
▷ Health: throat, kidneys, generative system, indirectly physical beauty.

MARS

Mars signifies war, courage and strength.

▷ Color: red
▷ Stones: ruby, bloodstone and red jewels
▷ Mars governs strength, courage, bravery, passion, self-reliance and anger.
▷ Health: the external head, the nose and smell, the generative system, the gall bladder, fevers, high temperature, infectious disease, eruptions, burns, scalds, bloodshed, sharp pains.

JUPITER

Jupiter signifies wealth, benevolence, philanthropy and sociability.

▷ Color: blue & purple
▷ Stones: turquoise, amethyst
▷ Jupiter governs harmony, wealth and benevolence. Good nature and a love of order.
▷ Health: feet, thighs, liver, blood, muscles, growth and digestion.

Saturn

Saturn signifies those aspects that relate to the earth, including mountains, hills, caves and even corpses and graves.

▷ Color: green
▷ Stones: Sapphire, obsidian, garnet
▷ Saturn governs the will and manifests as self-control, patience, reserve, austerity, chastity and practical ability.
▷ Health: bones, teeth, the spleen, diseases brought on by cold, rheumatism, falls, accidents, depression.

After you have successfully completed the 49 days of this meditation, you will have an internal solar system (at your solar plexus) to call upon in times of need. The solar plexus is the seat of your basic self and this constant source of light and energy will enable you to see any situation more clearly and will give you the strength to deal with that situation, resulting in more inner confidence and more control over outer situations. You can continue to use this as your daily meditation to concentrate on a specific element in your life, alternatively you can manifest the energies of all seven planets by imagining the ball radiating all their colors and energies outward throughout your body, giving you a rainbow-colored aura. If you need the energies of a particular planet, concentrate on its color and you will find that the energies of the other six stars will help you manifest that particular energy.

CONCLUSION

You should now have everything you need in your Book of Shadows to begin crafting your own spells. As we saw in Part 2, it is vital to work intuitively because that is how the spells you create will respond to your own personal energy. This means that, while it is good to read books to gain instruction initially, at some point you will need to put the books down and craft spells with your actions alone. This will come to easy to you once you have the confidence to do them.

It took me some time in life to gain the confidence I needed for creating my own spells. I was instructed for a time by a magician who would often just use whatever he had to hand to create a spell. So he barely even needed an altar or a Book of Shadows. You could try this, but I find that the psyche responds better initially to having a ritual and routine. The candle lit. The incense burned. The altar set up correctly. Then the spell recorded immediately afterwards so that you know what you set in motion and when, as you look for the seeds of change to begin bursting into life.

Having that repeating pattern in your magical life will enable you to very quickly step into the right frame of mind for creating and doing spells. Eventually you will find that as you go on walks in nature or spend time with friends, you will become attuned to the world around you. You will begin to sense when someone is not telling you what they are truly feeling and you will notice when nature is alerting you to changes that are happening. Stay alert and engaged and you will find that your spellcrafting is positively impacted.

The joy of becoming a seasoned practitioner is that you begin to walk lightly on your spiritual path. Your actions and values become aligned. You choose to do those things that support the world around you. You become a witch in the true sense of the word, helping those in your orbit and adding to the positive influences in the world through the gift of your magic.

One day you will awaken and find that you can sense energy in a way that you had never been able to before—through more than your main senses of sight, smell, hearing, taste, or touch. It will be a delight, but also requires you to trust in it and continue to pursue your magical work. Some find themselves afraid by the power they unlock in themselves. Don't be that person. This is your birthright. We are all witches at heart and we create magic every time we meet a goal, fall in love, attract good outcomes, and win at life. We just don't call it magic or say we're doing spells, but now that you are a spellcrafter, you know the truth. Enjoy your power freely, but with integrity.

Blessings to you and yours,

Silver Raven

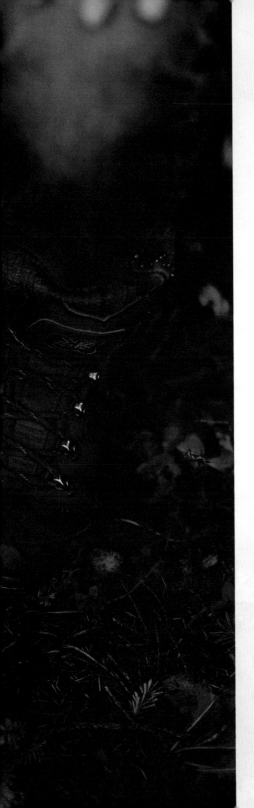

FURTHER READING

Spells, Charms, Talismans & Amulets – Pamela J. Ball (Arcturus, 2001)

Complete Book of Spells – Cassandra Eason (Quantum, 2004)

Vodou Shaman: The Haitian Way of Healing and Power – Ross Heaven (Destiny books, 2003)

The Element Encyclopedia of 5000 Spells – Judika Illes (Element, 2004)

Mastering Your Hidden Self: A Guide to the Huna Way – Serge Kahili King (Quest, 1996)

Charms, Spells & Formulas – Ray Malbrough (Llewellyn, 1986)

The Illustrated Signs and Symbols Sourcebook – Adele Nozedar (Harpercollins, 2016)

Oriental Magic – Idries Shah (ISF Publishing, 2019)

Egyptian Magic – E.A. Wallis Budge (Chartwell, 2016)